AF322980

BOOKS IN BLACK OR RED

Books
IN BLACK OR RED

By

EDMUND LESTER PEARSON

*"For him was lefere have at his beddes hed
Twenty bookes, clad in blak or red."*

Essay Index Reprint Series

BOOKS FOR LIBRARIES PRESS
FREEPORT, NEW YORK

First Published 1923
Reprinted 1969

STANDARD BOOK NUMBER:
8369-1267-5

LIBRARY OF CONGRESS CATALOG CARD NUMBER:
77-93371

PRINTED IN THE UNITED STATES OF AMERICA

"When Christmas comes about again,
    O, then I shall have money;
I'll hoard it up, and box it all,
    I'll give it to my honey:
I would it were ten thousand pound,
    I'd give it all to Sally;
She is the darling of my heart,
    And she lives in our alley."

PREFACE

"Why don't you write a book about book-collecting?"
said he.

"Well, the reason may seem a poor one," I replied,
"but I know no more about it than I do about operations
on Wall Street."

"But there must be a lot of poor birds," he persisted,
"who cannot buy rarities at hundreds of dollars apiece,
but like to acquire books at seventy-five cents or a dollar
or three. These fellows might like a book written expressly for themselves."

"They might," I admitted.

CONTENTS

ILLUSTRATIONS

THE LITERARY HOAX, I

BOOKS IN BLACK OR RED

CHAPTER I

THE LITERARY HOAX, I

Persons who have burned their fingers would be glad to have the literary hoax forbidden by law. Adventuring among books would be safer—and tamer. If it should be provided by statute that all books must follow their title-pages as exactly as a bottle of medicine must follow its label, our self-esteem would get fewer wounds, but our wits could be even duller. The traveller into the future, on H. G. Wells's "Time Machine," found men from whose lives all threats of danger, all but one, had been removed. Their life was safe, pleasant, and —mightily stupid.

Easy will be the work of the writer of book-reviews, and of his learned brother, the literary critic, when a hoax is punishable by fine and imprisonment. No band of conspirators will dare to unite in celebrating the life and works of an imaginary Russian novelist; the invention of a fictitious school of poetry, with samples of its style, will be as illegal as printing counterfeit treasury notes; all accounts of voyages to the South Seas must be narratives of fact. And then the writer of book-reviews may go away fishing or golfing, and leave still more and more of his work to his amanuensis.

The writer of a review is supposed to approach a book, not necessarily with suspicion, but at least with a question. Is it what it appears to be, or is it parody, or satire? Has this author ever visited the curious place which he describes, or known the poet whose strange verses he quotes? If the writer of reviews believes every statement he finds in print, and passes them on to his own readers, sooner or later he will get bitten. And then he accepts with good humor the joke upon himself, or else (if his self-importance is greatly over-developed) becomes furiously angry with the author, and denounces him in words of fire and brimstone.

"I have heard," said a Churchman of some rank—I think he was a Dean or an Archdeacon, for I remember that he reminded me of Trollope—"*I have heard* that that book is really *fictitious* from beginning to end!"

And he glared at me as if he intended to follow his remark with a medieval curse. I told him that I had heard the same thing and from good authority.

"Well!" he said, pounding the table, "the man who would do that is a hound! An absolute *hound!*"

I could not understand his wrath; the author's skill had aroused my admiration. But the Archdeacon's sense of devotion had been outraged. The book was "The Life of John William Walshe," by Montgomery Carmichael —one of the most inexplicable examples of the literary hoax. There are two outward signs of the biography as distinguished from the novel, as with many other books of fact compared with those of fiction: by some ancient convention it is supposed to be larger in size and higher in price. The Walshe book followed the latter of these requirements, unless I am mistaken, but not the former. Its size was that of a novel. It contained not one atom of satire, it was not a parody, and so far as I, at least, could have discovered by internal evidence, it was what it purported to be: a sober and reverent biography of an Englishman dwelling in Italy, a devout member of the Church of Rome, and in particular an enthusiastic student and pious follower of St. Francis of Assisi.

But John William Walshe, his ancestors and his family, his extraordinary literary labors, the close parallel of his saintly life to that of his exemplar, St. Francis, and finally his death, in the odor of sanctity and under the Papal blessing, were all of them invented by Mr. Carmichael—a member of the British consular service in Italy, and the author of a number of volumes, mainly works of *fact*. Why my Archdeacon could not have rejoiced at the creation of an imaginary character, whose piety he so much admired, is hard to explain, except on the ground that his self-esteem had been hurt because he had been fooled.

There is only the most distant relationship between the author of the literary hoax and the practical joker— that Eighteenth Century wag who thought it a devil of a fine trick to win a bet from his friends by some prank which inflicted physical pain or mental humiliation upon his victim. He was the spiritual grandchild of the medieval humorist. And he in turn, as he ran away with the miller's wife, never thought the cup of joy was really full unless the miller, reduced to his shirt, was left stuck fast in a bog, or wildly waving his heels from a snow-bank into which he had been plunged head first.

Theodore Hook was the type of the practical joker of a century ago, and the charming flights of his fancy may be appreciated by reading about his Berners Street Hoax, which is described, with similar triumphs, in Bram Stoker's interesting book "Famous Impostors."

Undergraduate hoaxes, at their best, are on a higher level of wit; they are frequently aimed at pompous beings in superior station, and for that reason could by no means be spared. The classic example is the famous Oxford "rag," when some students impersonating the "Crown Prince of Abyssinia" with his suite, were actually received on board H.M.S. *Dreadnaught* with proper salute of guns and all other ceremony.

In fiction, the college hoax is often elaborate, and designed for the mystification or embarrassment of one man. Thus, in Mr. E. F. Benson's story of Cambridge University, "The Babe, B.A.," it is a collegian with a snobbish reverence for royalty who is made to suffer pangs of jealousy by the spectacle of Queen Victoria herself, accompanied by a Lady-in-Waiting, entering another collegian's rooms to take tea. As the snob, fairly quivering with ecstasy and envy, breathes the prayer "God Bless Her!" he is wholly ignorant of the fact that he is imploring Divine favor upon merely a gifted member of the college dramatic club.

In one of Mr. C. M. Flandrau's uncollected stories, an undergraduate at Harvard, struggling under the burden of a sonnet which he has to write for a course in English composition, has wearied his classmates by his idea for an opening line. The tragic death of a great poet strikes him as a proper subject for his own first attempt at poetry; so he goes about asking everyone how the phrase "Shelley is dead!" would do as a beginning. He repeats the question so often that his friends take steps to inform him that they have heard enough about the lamentable event. His life, for weeks, is filled with reminders of the poet's death, but at last he comes to feel that humor has reached its limits. He is sitting in the Hollis Street Theatre, when an usher comes up with an urgent message requiring him to drive at full speed to the Massachusetts General Hospital. A cab takes him there in a few minutes; he arrives full of apprehension lest someone he knows may have been the victim of an accident. But on giving his name, he is handed a note by an unsympathetic nurse—a note which contains only the words: "Shelley is dead!"

"The Cobbler of Koepenick" should be added to Mr. Stoker's gallery of illustrious impostors. Morally he was no better than a swindler; the object of his masquerade was to loot a town treasury. His method, however—the assumption of a Prussian captain's uniform, which caused everybody to obey his orders—convulsed the whole world with laughter, and satirized German militarism as nothing else has ever succeeded in doing.

Such personages, however, are but distantly related to the author of a literary hoax. It is well to distinguish between the imposture (an ugly word with the suggestion of fraud for purposes of gain), the literary forgery and the literary hoax. There is a severe and ancient type of moralist who would put them all together in one batch—he would also throw in the novel, as a book containing nothing but "lies." I was shocked and amused, a few years ago, to find my name in the catalogue of the Boston Public Library, under the head: "Impostors— Literary." While I was wondering if this was an attempt at self-expression on the part of some acidulated cataloguer, I noticed that I was for once, and by the only possible method, in the distinguished company of Thomas Chatterton, and decided that I was being complimented beyond all deserving.

Time removes many fancied offences. Chatterton's persistence that he was not the author of the inventions which he put forward as the work of a medieval monk is as hard to explain as ever. But nobody sympathizes with Walpole's anger about it. Today Chatterton inspires wonder and pity—these and a vague belief that he was a great poet, driven to suicide by cruelty and neglect. I say a vague belief, because Chatterton is one of those literary figures whose name and fate are known to everyone, his writings virtually to no one. As Senator Lodge says,* "there is a general conviction that he was a genius, although it is doubtful if anyone except his editor or biographer could be found who could quote a line of his works." Except among professors of English literature, and not always with this exception, it would be perfectly safe to offer a reward to anyone who could offhand recite one stanza written by Chatterton.

He began, when fourteen, with the forgery of an

* In "Certain Accepted Heroes."

Chatterton's Holiday-Afternoon, by W. B. Morris

armorial blazon and a genealogical table to prove that one Mr. Burgum, a pewterer of Bristol, was a descendant of the noble family of De Bergham. (How could a pewterer be anything but absurd?) This tickled Mr. Burgum so much that he rewarded Chatterton with five shillings; probably it did not completely demoralize him, as the news did John Durbeyfield, the father of Tess, when the antiquarian told him that he was a member of the ancient and knightly family of the D'Urbervilles! But Chatterton's precocious talent and love of medievalism needed no five-shilling tips. There were left to him less than four years of life, but these were enough for the production of a considerable body of acknowledged poetry (far above the ability of the usual schoolboy) as well as the spurious works of "T. Rowlie," the Fifteenth Century priest, which provoked the extensive "Rowley Controversy," angered and confused some learned men, and fixed Chatterton's name as one always to be included in a history of English literature. Good critics find many passages of beauty and power in the Rowley poems; to me they are unreadable, and I am consoled to note that Palgrave omits Chatterton altogether from his "Golden Treasury." In more inclusive anthologies, however, the custom seems to be to give one example of his verse; this is the treatment accorded in such recent collections as Sir Henry Newbolt's "English Anthology," and in Mr. Le Gallienne's "Book of English Verse."

Before he was eighteen years old, hungry and in despair, Chatterton poisoned himself with arsenic—and died that most distressing death. His spirit came back, more than a century later, and stood beside another poet, Francis Thompson, and saved him from self-destruction. Thompson's reference to this may be found in Wilfrid Blunt's "My Diaries."

No form of literary hoax seems to leave a permanent legacy of anger or annoyance. No one thinks that Hawthorne was a fraud because he wrote, in the preface to his greatest novel, that he had discovered documents relating to Hester Prynne, together with the Scarlet Letter itself, in the attic of the Salem Custom House. Poe's balloon hoax is not counted against him today— it is little remembered—although it doubtless ruffled some readers of the New York *Sun* in April, 1844. They were avenged, by the way, more than sixty years later, when the *Sun* itself devoted more than a column of its editorial page to serious discussion of a literary hoax. Such writers as the ones I have mentioned, together with some lesser men referred to in the next chapter, perpetrated in various forms, the literary hoax. Their purpose was not to deceive anyone to his harm, nor were they seeking unfair gain for themselves.

Next come the literary forgers,—a different crew. These folk produce, say, some spurious manuscripts, supposed to be in the handwriting of a genuine literary man or historical personage. These they sell, under misrepresentation, to a wealthy collector. The victims may have recourse to law, but often they have to get along without sympathy. The most grievous case was that of the eminent French mathematician, M. Michel Chasles, who between 1861 and 1870 bought more than twenty-seven thousand forgeries, and paid out 150,000 francs for them.

A man with a meagre education, colossal assurance, and a strong right arm concocted these forgeries, and he must have worked at an average rate of about eight a day over a long period of years. His name was Vrain-Denis Lucas. The documents and letters included letters from Pascal (by the hundred), from Shakespeare (twenty-seven of them), hundreds from Rabelais, and others from Newton, from Louis XIV, from the Cid, from Galileo. But these were only the less remarkable items of the collection; the gems included letters from Sappho, Virgil, Julius Caesar, St. Luke, Plato, Pliny, Alexander the Great, and Pompey! There was a letter from Cleopatra to Caesar, discussing their son Cesarion; a note from Lazarus to St. Peter; and a chatty little epistle from Mary Magdalene to the King of the Burgundians. Why did he neglect to include the first A.L.S. recorded in history—the letter from David to Joab, which he sent by the hand of Uriah? Consider that these were all written on the same kind of paper, not on parchment, and that all of them, even those from Biblical personages, were written in *French*. Remember that they were eagerly purchased and their authenticity warmly defended, by one of the leading geometricians of his time, and then believe, if you can, that development of the mathematical faculty has anything to do with the reasoning power, or even with common sense.

In recent years, there flourished in Scotland one "Antique" Smith, who specialized in Scotch literary and historical manuscripts. A gentleman has told me that he remembers helping, with great care and reverence, to convey for the owner a portfolio of Smith's forgeries for inspection by another connoisseur and collector. For one of Smith's victims was a most worthy and benevolent gentleman, president of a famous American library. Not long afterwards, the imposture was discovered, and the villain went to his punishment—as you may read in "The Riddle of the Ruthvens," by William Roughead, a volume of fascinating essays on various kinds of rascality. You will thank me for telling you about it, even if you have to be at pains to secure it. To obtain some books requires a little more trouble than a telephone call to the nearest department-store. Though I shall have no objection if you can get this one of mine with no more effort than that.

As you and I do not belong to the class of young literary gentlemen (some of them are fifty-five!) who profess diabolism, and deny violently that they have any morals whatever, we are at liberty to shake our heads over the literary forgers, and pronounce them to be wicked men.

Yet Andrew Lang, in his "Books and Bookmen," writes of them with some toleration. They had to be clever, he admits. How young many of them were; how venerable and learned were the men they tricked! Lang thinks that the motives of the literary forger are curiously mixed, but that they are either piety, greed, "push," or love of fun. At first, literary forgeries were pious frauds in the interest of a church, a priesthood, or a dogma. Then came the greedy forgers, who were out merely for gain (Vrain Lucas?). Next the forgers who were inspired by what he calls "push"; they "hope to get a reading for poems, which if put forth as new, would be neglected."

A forgery by "Antique" Smith; Mary, Queen of Scots, to an
Edinburgh Printer

There is some reason for this belief; always there are readers who think more highly of a dull thing written three centuries ago than of any much more interesting but modern production. Some antiquarians, and probably more than a few book-collectors and experts on various bibliographical topics, belong, by the way, to this class. Never in their lives have they formed an opinion of their own about the merits of any book; literature is for them purely a matter of tradition, of other men's judgments. They can repeat the ancient catchwords, such as "old books are best," they can talk of "the safe judgment of time," and the "ephemeral character of present-day literature." As a matter of fact, they are merely lacking in taste and in courage; and are too dull ever to have an opinion by themselves. They care little for literature as a creative art, but are concerned solely with its mechanics. Discussing for hours a misplaced signature in a quarto "Hamlet," their faces become blank if someone mentions *Osric*. If the mistake is made of telling them who *Osric* is, their contempt for the man who is interested in such things is actually funny. They are embarrassed and frightened in the presence of creative work, but their intellects will grind and churn forever over the humdrum routine of some ancient printing house.

Finally, in Lang's classification, there are the forgers who are merely playful, or at least playful at the beginning. He places William Henry Ireland's Shakespearean forgeries (of which the best known is the tragedy of "Vortigern") in this class; while the Shakespearean forgeries of Payne Collier are more difficult to explain, and seem to have been the result of motives too mixed to be comprehensible. Sir Sidney Lee, it may be added, in his comments upon this subject, does not seem to have been impressed by the "playful" character of Ireland's and Collier's forgeries.*

Readers who look into Mr. J. A. Farrer's "Literary Forgeries" will find it an extensive treatment of this subject. Especially interesting is the chapter on George Psalmanazar, "the famous Formosan," who forged his name, the place of his nativity, and even the piety which so impressed Dr. Johnson. In Andrew Lang's introduction to Mr. Farrer's book there is an amusing recipe for those who wish to forge a Border Ballad, as well as a confession of the difficulties which he got into from his own minor and playful forgeries in writing his historical novel, "The Monk of Fife." He "forged" certain old records, he writes, with the result that the book confused a learned medievalist, who "could not make out whether he had a modern novel or a Fifteenth Century document in his hands, while the novel-reading public exclaimed, 'Oh, this is a horrid real history!' "

Even a forgery may be denounced with a severity out of all proportion to the harm which has been done. Sir Walter Scott was himself deceived by one of the numerous forgers of old ballads. But had he been undeceived, says Mr. Farrer, he would only have laughed. Sir Walter is quoted in Mr. Farrer's book as writing: "There is no small degree of cant in the violent invectives with which

---

* Mr. Lucas's book-dealer, Mr. Bemerton, in "Over Bemerton's," collected literary forgeries, and had actually read "Vortigern."

Charles Prince of Wales &c. Regent of Scotland
England France and Ireland and the Domin-
ions thereunto belonging. To our Trusty and
Well beloved

Greeting: We reposing especial trust and confidence
in your Courage and Loyalty and good Conduct
Do hereby constitute and appoint you to be a
Lieutenant of his Majesties Forces in the Regiment
commanded by   and to
take your Rank in the Army as such from the
Date hereof You are therefore carefully and dili-
gently to discharge the duty and Trust of Lieutenant aforesaid by doing and performing every
thing which belongs thereto and we hereby re-
quire all and sundry the Officers and Soldiers
to serve and obey you as Lieutenant and your
self to observe and follow all such Orders and
Directions as you shall from time to time receive
from us our Commander in chief for the time
being or any other your Superior Officer According
to the Rules and Discipline of Warr in pursuance
of the Trust hereby reposed in you: Given at Perth
this tenth of September 1745

Charles P. R.

Prince Charles commissions a lieutenant, by the hand of "Antique"
Smith

impostors of this nature have been assailed. If a young author wishes to circulate a beautiful poem under the guise of antiquity, the public is surely more enriched by the contribution than injured by the deception."

THE LITERARY HOAX, II

CHAPTER II

To those who have not stopped to think (and such persons exist, here and there, even among bookmen) the difference may not be apparent between the forgery and the hoax. It is, first and foremost, the spirit of the thing. The supposed value of the preposterous letters which Vrain Lucas sold to M. Chasles lay chiefly in the idea that they were in autograph. M. Chasles was so stupid that he deserves little sympathy; but Vrain Lucas was a swindler nevertheless—an uncommon swindler— and from a legal point of view, quite properly was sent to jail. The forger's motive was to make money.

But the "misleading" title-page of a hoax is seldom written in order to deceive the reader to his harm; there is no attempt to amass unlawful gain for the author; and, finally, it is a long-established literary convention. Its object may be playful; it may be "to give artistic veri- similitude to a bald and unconvincing narrative"; or it may be for reasons even more serious. A writer ven- turing outside his usual field may wish his readers to approach his book without preconceived opinions. The author's name may appear as editor. Sometimes the "deception" begins and ends on the title-page, in such conventional form as this: "Micah Clarke; his statement as made to his three grandchildren, *Joseph, Gervas,* and

Reuben, during the hard winter of 1734; wherein is contained A Full Report of Certain Passages in his Early Life, together with some Account of his Journey from *Havant* to *Taunton* with *Decimus Saxon* in the Summer of 1685. Also of the Adventures that Befell them during the Western Rebellion, & of their Intercourse with *James*, *Duke of Monmouth*, *Lord Grey*, and other Persons of Quality; Compiled Day by Day, from his Own Narration, by *Joseph Clarke*, & Never Previously set Forth in Print. Now for the First Time Collected, Corrected, and Rearranged from the Original Manuscripts by A. Conan Doyle. . . .''

Or the author's name may not appear at all: ''Personal Recollections of Joan of Arc by the Sieur Louis de Conte (her page and secretary). Freely translated out of the ancient French into modern English from the original unpublished manuscript in the national archives of France by Jean François Alden.'' Mr. Paine writes that Mark Twain said: ''I shall never be accepted seriously over my own signature. People always want to laugh over what I write and are disappointed if they don't find a joke in it. This is to be a serious book. It means more to me than anything I have ever undertaken. I shall write it anonymously.''

Yet as early in the Joan of Arc as the seventh page, there is a sentence which should have given, and probably did give, the clew as to authorship.

There have been three notable examples of the literary hoax within a few years. Each was justified by its wit, and any reader to whom this quality is not sufficient excuse for a book might find a still further defence in that the satire had a most useful effect. "Spectra; a Book of Poetic Experiments," by "Anne Knish" and "Emanuel Morgan" was published in 1916—when magazines, especially the freak magazines, were announcing the birth of some new "school" of art or poetry nearly every month. Most of these schools had the same relation to art that the Holy Rollers have to religion; they furnished amusement to the irreverent and unnecessarily troubled the extreme conservatives. The curious thing about these schools, cults, and coteries is the utter lack of humor with which they are acclaimed by their devotees and dupes. The extremists among those who sought freedom in art and literature soon passed over into anarchy; having thrown all rules of composition overboard, there was no good reason why a blotter upon which a bottle of red ink had been upset should not be framed and admired as a picture; while printer's "pi" could be—and in some magazines often is—printed and published as "poetry." Mr. Richard Aldington, in a review of James Joyce's "Ulysses," went further in honesty than most admirers of that book; he said that from the manner of Mr. Joyce to Dadaism is but a step and from Dadaism to imbecility is hardly that. Many of the reviewing periodicals, the "radical" ones, of course, in particular, in a fear of not seeming modern, surrendered their common sense and paltered with the good faith they owed their readers, by talking tolerantly and often with admiration about things which they knew were travesties of art. The publication of "Spectra" showed how easy it is to fall into a trap when merit counts for nothing compared with a supposed "novelty" or a spirit of revolt.

Two poets, Witter Bynner and Arthur D. Ficke, masqueraded as Emanuel Morgan and Anne Knish. Their Spectrist school of poetry arose from the name of a dance on a theatre programme: "La Spectre de la Rose." Having dined, and being in the mood which Milton allows to the lyric poet, Messrs. Bynner and Ficke took their cue from the word "Spectre" and there and then founded the Spectrist school. The elaborate explanation of the theory of their art, and the poems themselves, put forth under the heavy names of Morgan and Knish, resulted in an alarming rally of modernists and rebels. Letters and inquiries, praise for the new poetry, began to pour in. Then Mr. Ficke went off to the war, leaving Mr. Bynner with the whole school on his hands. He had to answer letters, sit at luncheons of poets and listen with a straight face to praise of the new "method." When the hoax was explained, some of the admirers and devotees added gratuitous amusement by sticking grimly to their guns, and insisting that the burlesque poetry was really very good, and that they had never been fooled, or that if they had, they were somehow right all the time. That is the advantage of abolishing all rules in art: nobody can ever prove you wrong on any subject.

The Spectrist school is dead, and like many other schools, dead or dying—Futurism, Vorticism, Cubism, Dadaism, Polyphonic Prose—it may not of itself have been humorous, but it was the cause of humor in others.

Gertrude Stein's "Tender Buttons"* is an extremely serious book, but its permanent value in literature (unless, as seems probable, it inspired large parts of "Ulysses") is that it provoked some of the best of Don Marquis's satire.

The authors and scholars who joined in celebrating the Larrovitch Centenary were so numerous that the resulting volume is probably unique. One or two originated the hoax, but a large group carried it on and perfected it. Designed at the beginning, I think I have heard, to rebuke the painful omniscience of one enthusiast in Russian literature, this little tribute is called "Feodor Vladimir Larrovitch; an Appreciation of his Life and Works." The editors are William George Jordan and Richardson Wright; it was published by the Authors Club of New York in 1918. To this volume Clinton Scollard contributed a sonnet, and there are scholarly essays and personalia about the great Russian by Professor Franklin Giddings and Dr. Titus Munson Coan. The bibliographies add to the charm of the book, but perhaps the most touching thing of all is the picture of "a pressed flower" from the grave of Larrovitch at Yalta, which is preserved and framed on the walls of the Authors Club. As with "Spectra," the hoax was inspired by a pose, a form of literary affectation; it cleverly satirizes the tendency in England and America to accept any Russian writer at whatever estimate some chortling enthusiast likes to put upon him. Max Beerbohm's "Kol-

---

* One of my prized first editions, picked up in the year of its publication for a mere song—fifty cents. Dr. Rosenbloom has more than once offered me sixty-five cents for it, but I shook my head. It was published in May, 1914. Some say it brought on the war.

niyatsch," in his book "And Even Now," is an earlier essay upon the theme. Kolniyatsch, the last of a long line of rag-pickers, acquired a passionate alcoholism at the age of nine, murdered his grandmother when he was eighteen, and spent the rest of his life in an asylum, writing poems and plays. His friends and relatives, as well as the officials, adopting the world's timid philosophy, called him insane, but Max Beerbohm, who was able to read his works in the original Gibrisch, would make no such clumsy classification.

But "The Cruise of the Kawa" was the most influential hoax of them all. Little pretence was made at the beginning; it was more a burlesque than a hoax. It absolutely put a stop to the flood of amorous South Sea books; nobody dared write in that vein afterwards. The picture of the nest of the Fatu-Liva bird carried the burlesque so far that the nature of the book instantly became apparent to anyone who chanced to open it at that point; some of the less farcical illustrations are more amusing. The portrait of Herman Swank is, to me, intensely funny, and the account of the customs of the dew-fish is perfectly written in a wistful vein of humor. Only one who has been connected with a literary hoax will be able to credit the statement that a man actually answered the advertisement in the back of "The Cruise of the Kawa," in which Dr. Traprock announces excursions to the South Seas. This man wished to inquire about passage on S.S. *Love-nest*, in order to "see the cute cannibals."

Only those behind the scenes in the production of a literary hoax can guess at the circumstances which may have led to its publication, or the curious incidents which follow. There are odd revelations of the human intellect and its operations, there is an exposure of that weakness to which we are all subject: the tendency to believe whatever we see in print. However much the author of a hoax may divulge afterwards, it is improbable that he will tell everything. He is sure to be a little aghast to discover how easy it is to deceive people—or rather, how apt they are in deceiving themselves. He cannot, if he has any heart or conscience, hold up all his victims on the point of his pen for the amusement of later readers; the sport is too much like pigeon-shooting at Monte Carlo. In the early days of the hoax, he is amazed to see unintended victims, walking blandly into the little net he has spread, quacking aloud at the same time, in order to advertise their entanglement. In a moment or two, they try to back out, bleating piteously—if I may mix my metaphors, in days when it is forbidden to mix anything stronger. If he goes to their help at this moment he is in danger of getting bitten. But he will notice, at the mouth of the net, a number of others, who had only been prevented from going in by the fact that there was no room. They are now pluming themselves on their perspicacity. The victims who have most cause for complaint will probably take the misadventure in good part; while those who rushed in uninvited may be annoyed. Their opinion of the hoax is that which the beetle holds of the electric light, as he sprawls in the dust below. "Drat the thing! What did they put it there for, anyhow? I was only doing my duty in trying to butt it over with my nose, but they never should have made it so hard!"

A hoax for which I was chiefly responsible left me with a bewildered feeling about antiquarian research and the writing of book-reviews. If I speak of it now at a length out of all proportion to its importance, and in conjunction with better books, it is because the experience showed me how little intent to deceive there may be in the origin of a hoax, and how readers often insist on hoodwinking themselves. Mine was published ten or twelve years ago, and is totally forgotten today. The model for it was "The Old Farmer's Almanack" whose quaint and amusing style has inspired so many imitations, and led Professor George Lyman Kittredge to write that entertaining volume, "The Old Farmer and his Almanack." I was writing, at that time, a newspaper column upon the subject of books and libraries, and it struck me that an old librarian might well have an almanac of his own, so I composed a paragraph in the manner of an imaginary book called "The Old Librarian's Almanack." It began with the customary warning: "About this time prepare for . . . etc." A controversy happened to be raging in the pages of *The Dial*—that excellent literary review, as representative of its day as its successor is of the tendencies of today. Unfortunately, no devotee of the modern *Dial* can ever see a copy of the paper as it was in that far-off year 1908, since to look back so far would be the deed of a reactionary. Somehow, the quotation from "The Old Librarian's Almanack" was injected into this *Dial* controversy, and presently a correspondent was found saying that he was quite familiar with the passage, intimating further that "The Old Librarian's Almanack" was an old favorite of his—the solace of his lonely hours!

Here was a painful situation—an honorable gentleman apparently professing familiarity with a book which had no existence! There seemed but one course open to any conscientious writer: to see that the book existed as soon as possible, in order to save the face of this admirer of it. So also thought Mr. John Cotton Dana, the librarian of Newark, and Mr. Henry W. Kent, librarian of the Grolier Club and now Secretary of the Metropolitan Museum of Art. They suggested that the Almanack become the first of a series of little books for librarians. With the moral support of these gentlemen—who were sporting enough to risk their money on the venture—and the typographical skill of the Messrs. Dana of the Elm Tree Press, the book was written and published. From the work of one Joseph Perry, who had published an almanac in New Haven in 1774, I shamelessly lifted all astronomical and meteorological details—all the hooks and eyes, curlicues and doodads, moons and stars, signs of the Bull, the Ram, and the Heavenly Twins. For all his literary productions I substituted my own, and it was rather a precise job of fitting lines, words and even letters into small spaces. From the printers it must have required much greater skill.

The point of the thing was this: it was designed to delude any intelligent reader for no longer than five minutes. It was purposely sown thick with anachronisms; its language was made unduly archaic; it contained innumerable clews of modern origin; and it ended with an outrageously farcical parody of an ancient cure for rattlesnake bite "made Publick by Abel Puffer of Stoughton." Abel Puffer, whose name falls as sweetly on the ear as Amos Cottle's, was a real personage who had actually written a rattlesnake recipe.

An early copy of the Almanack fell into the hands of an editorial writer on the New York *Sun*, who reviewed it for a column and a half, with no apparent doubt that its date was 1774, as the title-page set forth. A letter immediately sent by me to the *Sun*, and printed within the week, gave sufficient intimation of the modern authorship of the book. Yet, one by one, newspapers and literary reviews followed the *Sun* in gravely accepting my imaginary "Jared Bean," the crabbed Eighteenth Century librarian, as the author. One or two magazines or reviews were saved at the last minute from expressing similar pleasantly uncritical opinions. In some circles, where it became necessary to make a prompt decision about the antiquity of the book, amusing arguments and debates took place, some of the participants suggesting that the actual author was morally capable of such an act of turpitude, but not up to it intellectually.

Two months after I had myself set forth the nature of this transparent hoax, which as I have said, needed but five minutes' intelligent examination to be no hoax at all, the "discoveries" and "exposures" began. They continued for more than two years. I have a scrap-book full of data about this hilarious episode—printed articles, letters, telegrams, and other material, mostly good-natured, although occasionally irascible. These jests are too ancient to be retailed today, but looking at this scrap-book again, after a lapse of more than ten years, I am "filled with amaze." The "discoverers" of the modern origin of the Almanack balked at the name of the veritable Abel

Puffer, but swallowed the fictitious Jared Bean without a struggle. They became owlish about typography, paper, and the biographies of Eighteenth Century almanac-makers and printers. Light broke in upon them when they discovered obscure and recondite "clews"—of their own invention—after they had passed by a dozen obvious indications of modernity. They found jokes and allusions which were quite unknown to the author, just as the commentators on every writer from Shakespeare to Lord Dunsany have invented meanings of their own for various passages.* They found "really modern" expressions which, as a matter of fact, were not modern at all; they walked past signs which were wide as a church-door, to pick up microscopic imaginings of their own. One otherwise intelligent critic had a piece of bad luck; he chose the phrase "lose his guess" as a final clincher. That phrase was too modern to have been used a century ago, he said. It ought to have been so; I would have agreed to that myself, if I had not found "lose his guess" in a genuine almanac of 1774. The antiquity or modernity of phrases, especially of slang, is a dangerous subject upon which to be dogmatic.

The late Hamilton Mabie, after reviewing the Almanack in *The Outlook*, and reviewing it seriously, wrote to me that he had heard that all was not as it seemed to be; would I tell him if *The Outlook* was "again in the soup"? After I had told him my simple tale, he replied, saying in part: "The fact is, you caught me without angling. I

---

*In the face of Lord Dunsany's positive statement that there is no allegory in his plays, one of his critics stands up and flatly tells him to his face that he (the critic) knows more about it than the dramatist himself.

simply swallowed the bait whole. I hate not to be a game fish, but I would rather be truthful, so I am giving you the fact." He added an invitation which started me writing in a still different field, and had, at any rate, the effect of giving me an opportunity for amusing work for a number of years. When superior persons sneer at Mr. Mabie as a critic and writer, I am reminded of the fact that he had in him the instincts of a good sportsman in such matters, and lacked the pretence to omniscience which sours so much critical writing.

My firm belief that there were, on every page, enough indications of the origin of the Almanack, received a set-back when Sir William Osler wrote to Mr. Dana, three or four years later. He said: "I must say the Old Librarian's Almanack took me in completely. It was not until the other day that some friend suggested that some word —I have forgotten which—was not in use at that time. . . ." Possibly Sir William Osler's acquaintance with early books on medicine led him to accept a recipe which began by standing the patient upon his head! In a later letter to me from Oxford, in 1913, he wrote: " . . . I took a copy of the Almanack to the Colophon Club dinner last month. . . . To tell you the truth, you fooled us all. . . ."

I do not know what the customs of the Colophon Club may be, but I think that Jared Bean came up for examination after, and not before, dinner. Yet nothing could have been more ingenious than the *format* of the book as it was nicely planned by the editors of the series; while its typography won the praise of Theodore De Vinne himself. The wise folk who thought they found blunders in the non-literary parts of the book merely displayed their own ignorance. Any author should be proud to have his first book set forth with so much good taste and judgment.

Many men have invented a single imaginary book, or compiled the literary remains of an author who never existed. To have invented a private library, a collector of unique books, and actually to have issued a catalogue of a priceless collection of fictitious rarities, is a performance which only one man has ever attempted. He desired to play upon the book-collector's acquisitiveness, and to enjoy the spectacle of famous bibliomaniacs trying to steal a march upon one another. His success was stupendous, and the story of the hoax, even after more than eighty years, echoes from time to time in literary journals, and is familiar to some collectors. There are many, however, who seem never to have heard of it, and to the general reader it is unknown.

In 1840 there came by mail to book-collectors in Belgium, France, Holland, and England a sixteen-page pamphlet from which the title-page and other pages are reproduced here. It was printed in that town of Mons whose name, in August, 1914, was heard around the world. The sale, however, was at Binche. The prefatory note was a triumph of art—simple, touching, and above all, convincing. There is a certain dignified pathos in the reference to the owner of these wonderful volumes—

"Jean Népomucéne-Auguste Pichauld, comte de Fortsas," who was born at his château, near Binche, in Belgium, in 1770, and died in the same room "in which he first saw the light" in 1839. A marvellous collector, the Count! Devoted to his books, he had let the drums and tramplings of many conquests pass by, while he assembled his library of unique copies. *He would own no book of which any other copy existed.* No matter what price he had paid, let him find one of his books mentioned by a bibliographer, and he would sell, give away, or (*chose incroyable!*) destroy it! As a result, this collection, "very rich but few in number," represented a mere fragment of the Count's former library. The numbers in the catalogue ran up to 222, but there were many gaps, and only about fifty-two items actually appeared.

The poor Count had suffered some terrible blows. The publication of Brunet's "Nouvelles Recherches" was a heavy sorrow, making known, as it did, that there were other copies of many of his treasures. "Without doubt, it had in no small measure hastened his end." He had lost fully a third of his precious library at that time. The appearance of the various numbers of Techner's "Bulletin" still further depleted the ranks of his "sacred battalion," until there were, as I have said, only fifty-two items left to include in the catalogue.

But these items were of a kind to give a bibliomaniac a bad case of chronic insomnia. Conceived with devilish ingenuity so as to include some appeal to the whim of every famous collector of that day, the entries in the catalogue were forerunners of the ingenious titles which, many years after, Eugene Field liked to invent—as in his

CATALOGUE

D'UNE TRÈS-RICHE MAIS PEU NOMBREUSE COLLECTION

DE LIVRES

PROVENANT DE LA BIBLIOTHÈQUE

de feu M.^r le Comte J.-N.-A. DE FORTSAS,

dont la vente se fera à Binche, le 10 août 1840, à onze heures du matin, en l'étude et par le ministère de Me MOURLON, Notaire, rue de l'Église, n.º 9.

MONS,

TYPOGRAPHIE D'EM. HOYOIS, LIBRAIRE.

Prix : 50 Centimes.

"Temptation of Friar Gonsol."   There were titles in French, Latin, English, Dutch.   There were works which were supposed to have been totally destroyed, there were books throwing light upon obscure and mysterious historical events, there was an "infamous" satire against the Grand Monarch, there were "association" copies with autograph notes of famous men, there was a scandalous autobiography of an eminent prince, a *"catalogue plus que curieux des bonnes fortunes du Prince"* bound in "green chagrin, with a lock of silver gilt," which a horrified granddaughter frantically tried to bid in.   The Princess de Ligne, having no desire that the exploits of her ancestor should be published, or that the reputations of some of the ladies of the noblest families should suffer, wrote to M. Voisin to buy item 48 at any cost: *"Achetez, je vous en conjure, à tout prix, les sottises de notre polisson de grandpère."*   It is not clear from the catalogue that the Prince de Ligne was intended by number 48; there must have been reasons why the cap seemed to fit. There were other volumes of "piquant revelations" and "gallant adventures" which evidently caused uneasiness in various quarters.

During July, 1840, the bids began to come in to M. Hoyois, the printer and publisher of the catalogue.   The letters which accompanied the bids are amusing; most of the writers swallowed the bait and ran away with it. There were a few sceptics.   And there were a few cautious inquirers; they were partly credulous but would not say so; partly suspicious, but disliked to admit it.   They would not commit themselves to anything; they hoped to remain neutral in thought and word.   They did not know what was going to happen, but intended to be able to say "I told you so!" under any and all circumstances. These odd fish are always left high and dry, gasping on the bank, whenever a literary hoax is perpetrated. Some of them asked questions here and there, and received assurance that the Count's books were genuine, from experts who really knew as little as they. Some persons said that the books were not *all* unique; one gentleman asserted that he owned copies of several of them!

Mr. Arnold Lethwidge, writing about twenty years ago in the *Literary Collector*, gives a humorous account of the scenes in Binche on August 10, 1840, the day of the sale. Groups of strangers gathered in the streets, each carrying a copy of the little pamphlet. There were visitors from Brussels and Paris, from Amsterdam and London. They all wished to see "M. Mourlon, Notaire, rue de l'Église, No. 9." They snooped about, trying to avoid each other. When one book-collector met an acquaintance he muttered something to the effect that he was merely passing through, on his way to Brussels. They gathered at the inn, and bewildered the inn-keeper and natives by their persistent inquiries about M. Mourlon.

The stage from Paris arrived, bringing a dozen more visitors. The great French bibliographer, Brunet, was there, so was Nodier, and the Baron de Reiffenberg, director of the Royal Library of Belgium. He had asked for a special appropriation to enable him to buy some of the treasures, omitting from his list, however, certain items, as "too *free* for a public library." Eager buyers had come from England; the Roxburghe Club had sent a representative.

malheur pour sa gloire, le Conseil fut avis de cette édition clandestine; et, comme quelques perruques de ce respectable corps étaient assez mal traitées dans ses rimes, on fit saisir le livre avant qu'il eu vu le jour. Mon exemplaire, seul échappé à la brûlure générale provient des héritiers de l'auteur.

Poisson était aussi célèbre par ses calembours que par ses vers; et pour finir dignement, comme il avait vécu, il voulut finir par une pointe. Pendant qu'on lui administrait l'extrême-onction : « Pauvre Poisson, s'écria-t-il, tu es f....., on t'accommode à l'huile. »

38 Evangile du citoyen Jésus, purgé des idées aristocrates et royalistes, et ramené aux vrais principes de la raison, par un bon sans-culotte. Arras, an m de la République une et indivisible, in 12 de 168 pages, volume inachevé.

Ce volume, qu'il ne faut pas confondre avec l'évangile Toucquet, est l'œuvre du fameux Joseph Lebon. Je tiens mon exemplaire de M.r Du Rbin, d'Arras, qui l'avait soustrait, chez l'imprimeur, à la destruction totale de l'édition restée inachevée à la chute du féroce évangéliste de la Convention.

40 Mémoire justificatif des P. P. de l'oratoire de Jésus de Mons, indignement accusé d'hérésie; où l'on démontre la turpitude et les intrigues de leurs ennemis, petit in-4.°, sans lieu ni date, de 94 p.

Très-curieux, et contenant une foule de personnalités contre les membres du Magistrat d'alors (1600 environ). Bayle, dans ses lettres, regrette de n'avoir pu se procurer ce piquant factum.

43 Les suites du plaisir, ou desconfiture du Grand Roi dans les Pais Bas. Au Ponent (Hollande), 1686, in-12, 152 p., fig., mar. noir, doré s. tr.

Libelle d'un cynisme dégoûtant à l'occasion de la fistule de Louis xiv. Une des figures représente le derrière royal sous la forme d'un soleil entouré de rayons, avec la fameuse devise : Nec pluribus impar.

46 Les géorgiques du cygne mantouan, translatées du latin virgilian et reduis en ryme françoise. Ensemble un discours non moins recréatif à qui tiltre est, Le Malvoisin, par Libert Houthem, Ilgeois. A Mons en Haynau, chez Rutgher Velpius, 1580, in-8.°, vu 128 p.

Encore un oublié par M.r Vanhasselt. Houthem est connu par d'autres ouvrages.

47 Disputatio philosophica, qua anonymus probare nititur homines, ante peccatum, sexum non habuisse. Coloniae Allobr. apud J. Tornaisium, MDCVII, in-4.°, 48 pp. figures, demi-reliure, non rogné.

Cet ouvrage a appartenu à Liebnitz, dont il porte la signature et plusieurs notes autographes.

48 Mes campagnes aux Pays-Bas, avec la liste, jour par jour, des forteresses que j'ai enlevées à l'arme blanche.

Imprimé par moi seul, pour moi seul, à un seul exemplaire, et pour cause.

A. B., de l'imprimerie du P. Ch. De —

Sans année, in-8.°, 208 p. relié en chagrin vert, avec fermoir à clef, d'argent doré.

Catalogue plus que curieux des bonnes fortunes du Prince. Le maréchal de Richelieu lui avait sans doute donné l'idée de ce singulier inventaire.

50 Il pentamerone del cavalier Giovan Batista Basile, ouero lo Cunto de li cunte Trattenemiento de li Peccerille di Gian Alesio Abbattutis. In Amsterdam, presso D. Elsevier, 1675, in-12, vel.

52 Hystoire tres plaisante et recreative du noble chevir, le gentil seigneur Gil de Chyn, lequel fist moult grant procex oultre mer. On les vend à Paris en la grand salle du palais, au premier pillier, en la boutique de Galliot Dupre, marchant libraire de l'Université de Paris. MDXXXI, petit in-f.°, goth., à 2 col. 84 feuillets; veau brun.

53 Brouet confortatif pour les âmes foibles en dévocion; ensemble un brief discours en forme de consolacion touchant les misères de ce temps, par Charles de Hainin licentié es droits. A Tournay chez Adrien Quinquet, MDCXXXI, in-12, 131 pp. maroquin vert, dor. s. tr. (Tournais.)

From the Fortsas Catalogue

These strangers and their curious behavior began to make the people of Binche uneasy. The police were worried; it was a time of unrest in Europe, and the authorities were always suspecting outbreaks and revolutions. Were these odd-looking men, with their stooped shoulders, and their little pamphlets, dangerous characters in disguise? Might they not be planning an *émeute?* No little town ever thinks of itself as anything but the centre of the world—was the peace of Europe about to be shattered again, and had Binche been selected as the place to touch off the explosion? They all talked, did the strangers, of M. Mourlon, the notary, of the Rue de l'Église, and the Comte de Fortsas. There was no Rue de l'Église, and no notary named Mourlon; the citizens knew nothing of a Comte de Fortsas. The day wore on, and still the bibliomaniacs raged in the streets.

A quiet gentleman who had come in on one of the earlier stages followed the book-collectors about, and listened to their talk in the inn. When the evening stage arrived from Brussels, he wandered over and took from it one of the newspapers which it brought. Then he sprang a surprise. He read aloud an announcement. The town of Binche, moved by local pride, had bought the entire collection of the Comte de Fortsas, to be preserved entire, and to be kept there. So there would be no sale. At this, the excitement broke out; arguments, expostulations, complaints, and still further enquiries addressed to the town officers. Why had they not been notified? Why had they been allowed to come so far for nothing? It was infamous! But, Messieurs, persisted all the folk of Binche, we have bought no rare books, we do not own any books; there is no M. Mourlon, there is no Comte de Fortsas; we have never heard of such persons.

"It is all a hoax, then!" suggested somebody. And someone else wondered if the quiet man who had read the notice in the Brussels paper could tell them anything more about it. They looked for him, but he had disappeared. They never found him again. He was M. Renier Chalon, an antiquarian and a writer of books on numismatics. He had invented the Comte de Fortsas and his library, had written the catalogue out of his own imagination, knowledge of books, and of the weaknesses of his fellow collectors, and had taken his pay in riding to Binche with the bibliomaniacs, watching their maneuvers to outwit each other, listening to their discussion of these imaginary works, and hearing one or two of them claim that they also owned copies of some of the best items in the Count's library!

"It was," says Mr. Lethwidge, "an admirable jest, perfectly carried out, causing discomfiture to many, distress to none." After the famous tenth of August had gone by a cloud seems to settle upon the whole affair. Collectors who were present did not widely advertise the fact. The wise ones who had claimed to own some of the Count's books, suddenly became silent about them. The cautious probably boasted that they had been suspicious all the time. They are alike in all ages! Some literary journals referred to the "mystification." The whole truth seems not to have come out for nearly sixteen years, when M. Hoyois, the printer of the catalogue, published an extensive account of the matter, giving the letters which

he had received. This act cost him the friendship of
M. Chalon.

A copy of the catalogue of Count de Fortsas' library
was bought at the Poor sale in New York for $40. It
was Baron de Reiffenberg's copy with his annotations.
There are reprints of the catalogue which turn up for sale
now and then. They are pleasant reminders of the most
successful and ingenious literary hoax of all time. Others
have deceived or amazed a certain number of persons,
and have had amusing results. This alone was dynamic.
One still delights to picture the dusty streets of the
Belgian town on that far-off day in August; the bewildered townsfolk; the book-collectors from the cities in
their long-skirted coats and top hats, all of them eager but
sly, furtive, puzzled, but above all greedy to lay their
hands upon the treasures collected by M. le Comte de
Fortsas.

BOOK-SHOPS

CHAPTER III

"The proper sort of book-shop," began **B.**,

"Is a second-hand book-shop," interrupted **F.**

"Oh, I'm tired of all you sentimentalists talking about old book-shops! If you really want to get a book, and to get it today, you go to the biggest book-store in town. And that's usually a shop devoted to new books. If you are looking for something to write about, like all these fellows who are bent on being so whimsical and charming, of course a second-hand book-shop is your place."

"I am thinking," F. returned, "about buying books as an art rather than as a science; about pleasure *versus* business. The hunt is what makes the fun, as in everything. If eating two or three skinny trout were all a man got out of going fishing, who would take the trouble? It's like getting married: which do you sympathize with—the man who takes care that his income is all right, and then coolly looks about for a suitable person, and maybe advertises for her; or with the poor, sentimental fish who meets someone quite unexpectedly, finds that life is intolerable without her, and so rushes ahead into marriage? You may call it sentimentalizing, but there is some sport if you wander into a book-shop, merely to moon about, and perhaps stumble upon something good. If you dash in to get a particular book, and instantly have it wrapped up, you may as well be buying a turnip."

He paused; but the rest of us did not feel controversial, so he filled his coffee-cup again and continued.

"If you expose yourself to the contagion of books, the results may be interesting. That was a satisfactory book-shop in 'Over Bemerton's.' "

"What was it like?"

"I forget. But somebody lived above it—which must have been handy. And he bought of Mr. Bemerton a copy of Giles's 'Chinese Biographical Dictionary.' That alone would make any book-shop memorable."

"The right kind of a book-shop," began R., this time.

"Your idea," interrupted B., "is one full of first editions of Lafcadio Hearn, Anatole France, and George Moore, lying in a tray marked: 'Take Your Pick, 35 cents.' The book-seller would be old, partly blind, and hopelessly crippled."

"That is, in the main, correct," R. agreed; "except that they would be marked 5 cents instead of 35."

"But where is the joy of pursuit, of hunting down the prize—where is even the mercenary joy of bargaining with the dealer."

"Nowhere," returned R. "I would forego these things. I would be out for plunder. For the pleasure of possessing these treasures; showing the books to my friends, and hearing them (to quote Eugene Field) wail to know I got them cheap."

The proper sort of book-shop is on a side street. It has to be; rents elsewhere are too high for the modest book-seller. The great whales of his profession, those who minister to the criminally rich, may exist on the main streets. The streets which you remember with affection, the streets which attract when first you discover them and linger pleasantly in your mind, are always side streets. The Kalverstraat, in Amsterdam, is the great type—and you can shake hands across it, from sidewalk to sidewalk. Are there any book-shops on it? I forgot to look. Somebody tells me that there is a narrow street near the Mitre in Oxford, and that it is equipped with a book-shop.

The proper sort of book-shop is in an old building; it is old and dingy itself. Dingy, but not dirty nor dusty. It is not necessary to have your shop in such a condition that your customer, after four minutes' poking about, has to go to a Turkish bath. There is a shop in New York, of which the proprietor has a patriarchal Old Testament name, where they are devotees of the dirt theory. They must bring it in on shovels, and sprinkle it over the books. And their prices are no lower than elsewhere. I came out from under a heap of books one day, looking like a sweep, only to learn that the principal pirate was going to charge me—but this is not a recital of atrocities.

The shop ought to be high and rambling, though it need not be large. There are not so many interesting books in the world. Big book-shops are full of plugs. But it should be packed with books, up to the high ceiling, and there should be dim corners in it, and unexpected turnings and out-of-the-way shelves, so that there may be surprises, and arcana, and mysteries. You must not be able to comb the place at your first visit. You should leave with the intention of coming back, and having another squint at the top shelves, or at some recess which the light did not reach on the rainy day when you first came.

There should be one or two (one is best) unobtrusive clerks,—or better, the dealer himself, as he has the right to reduce prices—and a few (a very few) well-behaved customers, who keep out of your way. Smoking should be permitted. It is, in most shops. There is, also in New York, a shop on Vesey Street, with a large sign forbidding smoking! I would say that this is a bad shop— except for the fact that I got a clean copy of Anstey's "Salted Almonds" there for fifty cents. By virtue of being on a top shelf it had escaped notice amid a mass of commonplace novels.

A dim recollection comes to me of a shop in London, near St. Paul's, which had room for exactly one customer at a time. It was a little gem of a shop, not much larger than a sentry-box, but with its walls lined with books to eight feet above the floor. I was a little embarrassed, however, by the presence of the First Lord of the Treasury, or at least the Secretary of State for Foreign Affairs. Such, from his dress, his dignified countenance, and his deportment, I imagined the frock-coated gentleman to be. He remained seated, and in the half-light I stumbled over his feet. After courteously acknowledging my apologies, he inquired if he could serve me. He was the proprietor!

The embarrassment was all on my side when, a few moments later, I placed eighteen-pence in his palm in return for a small book. He bowed with complete gravity, but I felt like the man who absent-mindedly tipped the Papal Nuncio.

For its physical characteristics, there is in New York no shop which lives up to my specifications better than one on—but I had best not give advertisements. I will say, for the literary detective, that the name of the street is that of one of England's queens, that the street number is the title of a novel by Booth Tarkington, and the proprietor's name is rich in romantic suggestion of old Spanish Jewry. I cannot imagine a better name for a bookseller—for I am under no delusions about business dealings with the descendants of Abraham and Isaac. I will entrust myself to their mercy as quick as to Yankee or Briton, and be fleeced as often by one as by the other. And not often by any of them. Except a few extortioners—and these, I think, among the great Napoleons of the tribe, who despoil the plutocrat, or sell limited editions to the parvenue, book-sellers are as honest as any other men. It may be rash, but I'll risk the assertion.

This shop, in appearance, is all that may be desired. And the best restaurant in the lower part of the city is on the same narrow street. You may go in there and sit and eat until gorged to repletion, then come forth, cross the street, and fumble about the dark and attractive shelves of the shop whose name and address are alike romantic. When I found in it a good, early edition of "Sylvie and Bruno," which became my property for seventy-five cents, I thought I had discovered the place of my dreams. But nothing so agreeable to my whims has appeared there since.

Another shop, whose lure is wholly on the outside, is in a neighborhood once associated with Mr. John Masefield, and still the murmurous haunt of poets, playwrights and novelists. On warm summer evenings the clicking of their typewriters rises in chorus to the stars. It is said that the poet tried this shop and liked it not. Its signs always make me stop. Here is one of them:

BOOKS ON ALL SUBJECTS

Rare and Curious Books
Wit Humor Proverbs
Funny Limerick Jokes
All the poets from
"Homer" & "Virgil" to "Kipling"
Apocryphal old &
New Testaments
Prayer Books Bibles
Renan's Life of Jesus
Face on the Bar Room Floor
Oriental Religion &
Scotch Clans and Tartans
How to become a Citizen
Oscar Wilde G B Shaw
Gilbert's Bab Ballads
Theosophy Spiritualism
Psychology Mythology
New Thought Plato
Vest Pocket Editions
Ruskin Sea Yarns
Irish Scotch and other Toasts
Fortune Telling Cards
Rhyming Dictionaries
Roget's Thesaurus
"Albertus Magnus" Magic
Birthday Horoscopes
Gold Fountain pens 1.00
Irish Scotch and old Songs
Brann's "Iconoclast"
Schopenhauer's Essays

Freemasonry   Oddfellowship
Dream Books   Sexology
Tell your Friends

A second sign informs you that the shop has "½ a million books on all subjects" and the shop is 110 feet deep. Still another announces

IRISH BOOKS OF ALL KINDS

Kickham's "Knocknagow"
The Koran 1.50 The Talmud 1.50
Fortune Telling Cards & Books
Pepys' & Evelyn's Diaries
The Chef's Reminder
How to save Your Child's Life 1.00
6th & 7th Book of Moses
Chesterfield's Letters   Typewriting
Moody's and other Sermons
Josephus Confucius
Astrology   Palmistry
Care of Dogs Birds and Pets
Tom Paine   Ingersoll
Sinking of the Titanic
After Dinner Stories Law
How to be Beautiful
How to be a Detective
Wild Flowers Trees Birds
Old Magazines   Bridge
Dress Making Millinery

But when you enter the illusion is broken. If you know exactly what you want, all is well. But whoever does know exactly what he wants in a second-hand book store? They are not made for such definite people. And if you wish to look about, you raise suspicion in the breasts of the proprietors. It must have happened, one day, that somebody in the deepest recesses of that 110 foot shop, tried to fill his pockets with some of the half million books, and creep nefariously forth. At any rate, customers are under a thick cloud of distrust.

There once was a place on Fourth Avenue, where you could descend into an evil hole, warmed by the flames of the pit,—all atmosphere was unknown save the asphyxiating fumes of an oil stove. Here gathered certain crapulous old men to claw over the European novels.

Very different is Mr. ————'s shop near Fifth Avenue. It is swept and garnished: it contains many fine books, and Mr. ———— with the graciousness of an Ambassador, will sell you a good honest copy of a book, for, say, five dollars. True it is that some other dealer, a few blocks away, will sell you one exactly as good for two dollars and a half. But atmosphere is certainly something, and so is tradition, and the feeling that no vulgar purchase, but a diplomatic causerie, is forward.

Experimenting with them all, and not ignoring the attractions of the one with the romantic address, I am left with a strong prejudice in favor of a small shop I came upon by accident. Following my custom, I will disguise the avenue on which it stands by saying that it has the name of a town where minute-men once gathered on the green, one April morning, to begin a great war. And although the proprietor has called his shop after some bird—robin or wren—his own name will remain darkly hidden if I say that one of this patronymic wrote the "Elegy on the Death of a Mad Dog." A little dog is one of the inmates of the shop, which is remarkable for a small but choice collection of books. The proprietor is one of those unusual beings who reads, and yet has not an exaggerated idea of the value of books. Many of the dealers seem to be bitten with the "first edition" craze— they talk about first editions of this writer and that, till one may expect to hear of first editions of Harold Bell Wright.

Buying second-hand books is as interesting a game as poker; not as exciting, but never so expensive. It has the fascinations of discovery and exploration. You are always about to happen on something that you greatly desired. Beyond the horizon is the prize—and it is a horizon that fades forever and forever as you move. The pot of gold is at the rainbow's end, and you never catch up with it. But you keep finding pieces of gold which have fallen out. You do not go after any book in particular—if you play the right game—but you have vague recollections of forgotten books which you would gladly see again. Or you discover fascinating things which are totally new to you. The rivalries and enmities of the dealers are quaint, and the eccentricities of collectors as merry as the cantrips of unicorns on a grassy plain.

By E. B. Bensell, in Stockton's "The Floating Prince"

WIZARDS AND ENCHANTERS

By J. G. Francis, in *St. Nicholas*

CHAPTER IV

In "African Game Trails" Mr. Roosevelt said that he was "in a bond of close intellectual sympathy" with the Doctor of the expedition, "ever since a chance allusion to 'William Henry's Letters to His Grandmother' had disclosed the fact that each of us, ever since the days of his youth had preserved the bound volumes of *Our Young Folks*, and moreover firmly believed that there never had been its equal as a magazine, whether for old or young, even though the Plancus of our golden consulship was the not wholly happy Andrew Johnson."

It is true, as Mr. Roosevelt implies, that no agreement about books, not even in the vexed question of sea-stories, can make us look upon another man with so friendly an eye as the discovery that he belonged to our period, and shared our especial enthusiasms about reading, in the years that stretched between the sixth birthday and the sixteenth. There may be endless debate as to the best period, the best authors, and the best magazine. There was the age of Mayne Reid and Oliver Optic, of Castlemon and Trowbridge, of Henty and the others who followed. The two African hunters, who happened to be young when Andrew Johnson was President, may insist on the superiority of *Our Young Folks*; men of later decades will be equally firm for *St. Nicholas*, for *The Argosy*, for *Golden Days*, for *Harper's Young People* or for *The Youth's Companion*. The decades overlap; the really excellent authors do not go out of favor with the first generation; we read some of the books, at least, and sometimes the very copies, which our fathers enjoyed. And bound volumes of magazines descend to us, to our delight, from older brothers and sisters. But the magic time of children's books is our own youth, and fortunately for children, it begins anew,—the golden years return.

It must be enjoyed while it lasts, for it slips away from each generation in order to visit the next. But for those who have left the wonderful years behind, it returns no more. We shall never get that thrill again. I do not, customarily, nowadays, run half a mile down the street to meet the postman and relieve him of a magazine for which I have been feverishly waiting for a whole month; nor walk two miles to get the seventh chance at a book for which six others are also impatient. But I can recall a time when such proceedings seemed altogether natural and proper. I am afraid I shall never again find the books that will convulse me with laughter, or turn my spine into one long icicle, as once they could do. And there are folk who pride themselves on exactly this insensitiveness, this sophistication!

Although I know that the golden age of children's books is repeated over and over again; and that the wonder bursts upon each generation, without regard to any group of writers, or any single children's magazine, I find myself pitying the boys of today. Poor little devils —they haven't the books I had. Those whose "golden consulship" is that of Wilson or Harding are out of luck, compared with us of the days of Cleveland and Harri-

creased size. Twice as big! To the round eyes gazing at them they looked as big as the barn, and if any little reader doubts it, let him measure twice the length and breadth of his boot, and put his foot upon the measure.

Tears could no longer be kept back. Tinkey kicked the shoe into the corner of the room with a passionate sob.

"I wont go!" he cried. "I wont wear my old trousers and shoes with a great patch on them!"

"Are you never coming?" shouted Bob from down-stairs.

"I 'll walk over! Don't wait for me!" Tinkey answered, and could hear them all laugh as Fannie said:

"Tinkey 's prinking! Wont he be fine!"

Should he go? Mrs. Davidson's annual party was not to be lightly set aside, and was one of the great pleasures in Tinkey's quiet country life. Perhaps among so many his dress would not be noticed, and he had not seen some of the boys since

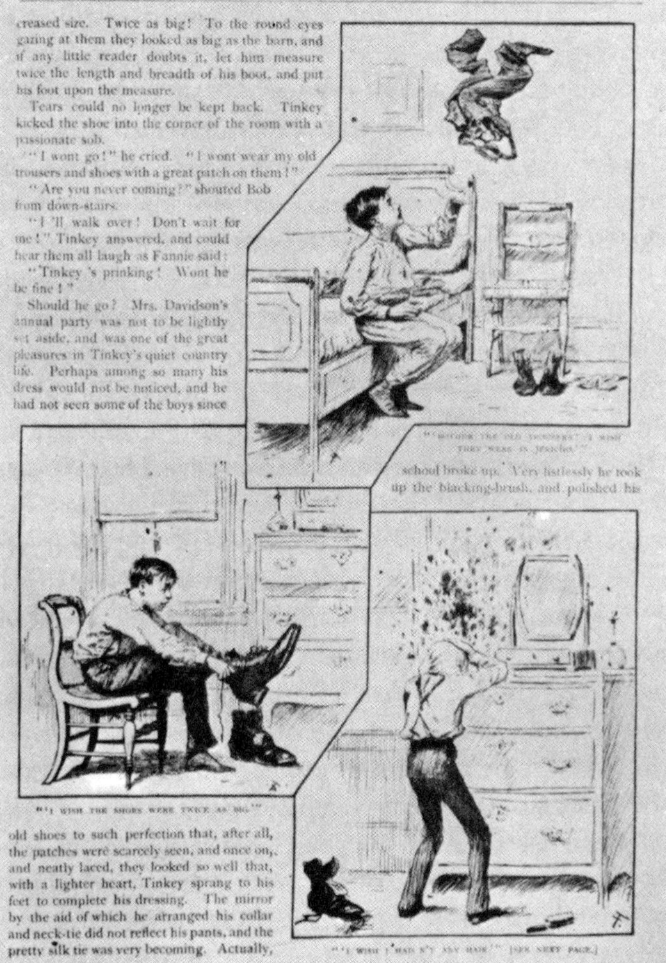

school broke up. Very listlessly he took up the blacking-brush, and polished his old shoes to such perfection that, after all, the patches were scarcely seen, and once on, and neatly laced, they looked so well that, with a lighter heart, Tinkey sprang to his feet to complete his dressing. The mirror by the aid of which he arranged his collar and neck-tie did not reflect his pants, and the pretty silk tie was very becoming. Actually,

By A. B. Frost in *St. Nicholas*

son.   And when I try to explain why this is so I find myself thinking constantly of one author and the title of one magazine: Frank Stockton and *St. Nicholas*. The writings of Frank Stockton are, of course, available for children today, and read by them. But his name represents, to me at least, a group of authors and artists who charmed the readers both young and old of 1880 to 1887, odd, humorous, gentle, creators as they were, of all kinds of fancies and conceits. They were masters of a clear narrative style, writers of good English. They did not have to depend upon the last up-to-the-minute topic, nor turn out to order, yarns about "Aeroplane Boys" and "Radio Boys."   And when a notable success is made today in writing books for children—as in Mr. Bowen's "The Old Tobacco Shop" or Mr. Lofting's "Story cf Dr. Dolittle"—I notice that it is to Frank Stockton or to Charles E. Carryl, the other great name of that period, to whom we go for comparison by way of praise.

We are breeding, among American authors today, any number of clever satirists, some of whose writings are a most wholesome medicine; we are also training a crew of little Russians, tiresome ninnies, to whom the sour stomach is prerequisite for great literature. There must be thousands of readers who do not wish the syrups of an absurd optimism, but who equally have no desire for the wormwood of an affected pessimism. They do not, in short, wish to be medicined at all when they open a book, but to be amused. At present, they are confronted by a chorus of terribly serious, humorless men, who are pounding on the table, and growling portentously: "You wish to be amused, do you? By Godfrey! you shall not be amused; we're going to set your teeth on edge!" And such readers, remembering Frank Stockton's stories and novels for adults, naturally wish for another like him.

St. Nicholas goes on its way, as it used to do, amusing and pleasing children, and coming out each year in bound volumes with the morning-glories on the cover. For me, however, the great years are those of the 1880's. Not long ago I acquired, from a noble book-seller, fifteen or twenty of the volumes, and on the day after their arrival —a Sunday—the strange spectacle could be observed of three or four doddering old men of forty or thereabouts, sitting on the floor at my home, lost to all sense of propriety, and totally neglectful of such sane and decent topics of conversation as politics, business, or prohibition. For two hours or more nothing could be heard but: "Here's the poem about the De Gustibus:

> On the edge of the wood
> A De Gustibus stood
> With a gentle expansible smile——"

Or "Here's the picture of the Aristocrats winding up the city,—by George! I haven't seen that for thirty years!" Or "Here's 'Phaeton Rogers'—I read that twelve times."

This was the period when Frank Stockton's best tales were appearing: "The Floating Prince" and "How the Aristocrats Sailed Away" and "The Castle of Bim," with its engaging character, the Ninkum, who liked to lie on his back, gaze up at the sky and expand his mind. These stories were illustrated, some by E. B. Bensell and some by Reginald Birch, and no one who read them has ever

From *St. Nicholas*

forgotten the pictures,—they are as familiar, as well-beloved, and as essential to the story as Sir John Tenniel's illustrations for the "Alice" books. The story of "The Griffin and the Minor Canon," perhaps the nearest to perfection of them all, so impressed me with the dietary habits of Griffins—"I never eat between the equinoxes. At the vernal and at the autumnal equinox I take a good meal, and that lasts me half a year"—that never to this day do March 21 or September 21 come around, that I do not remember to beware of Griffins. Mr. Bensell was the illustrator of Carryl's "Davy and the Goblin," and drew the immortal picture of the Cockalorum.

It was an age of excellent nonsense verse; not so much talk was made about it as at a later date, but more of it was written. The pages of *St. Nicholas* were full of it. There was "The Carnivoristicous Ounce" by Mrs. M. E. Blake, verses which the attractive young hero of Frank Norris's "Blix" was fond of quoting:

> There once was a beast called an Ounce,
> Who went with a spring and a bounce;
>   His head was as flat
>   As the head of a cat,
> This quadrupedantical Ounce
>   'Tical Ounce,
> This quadrupedantical Ounce.
>
> He sprang on his prey with a pounce,
> And gave it a jerk and a trounce;
>   Then crunched up its bones
>   On the grass or the stones,
> This carnivoristicous Ounce,
>   'Ticous Ounce,
> This carnivoristicous Ounce!

There was the "Untaught Sea-Urchin" and also:

> There once was an Ichthyosaurus,
> Who lived when the earth was all porous,
> But he fainted with shame
> When he first heard his name,
> And departed a long time before us.

Walking through Union Square one afternoon, a year or two ago, and talking with my companion about these *St. Nicholas* days, we spoke of J. G. Francis, his marvellous pictures of animals, and the rhymes and jokes which accompanied them. I tried to recall the one which always pleased me most, but could not remember it, except in bits. I wonder if I were not walking with the only man in New York that day who could have recited it, instantly and correctly? It was Arthur Guiterman, and he quoted:

> A Tam o' Shanter Dog
> And a plaintive piping Frog,
> With a Cat whose one extravagance was clothes,
> Went to see a Bounding Bug
> Dance a jig upon a rug
> While a Beetle balanced bottles on his nose.

Not Guiterman, no, and not Swinburne, ever composed a line more delicious than that last one about the Beetle, although either of them would have shied at the rhyme of *nose* and *clothes*. It used to vibrate in my ears like sweet music and it does still. Mr. Francis' cats, rabbits, sheep, and best of all, his ducks and geese, are not denied to children today, for his "Book of Cheerful Cats" is issued in edition after edition. The same artist also made

Copyright by *The Century Co.*

By J. G. Francis, in *St. Nicholas*

the curious old Mexican pictures, the "Aztec Fragments" which were appearing in *St. Nicholas* in '87 and '88.

One other haunting memory centred about a page of pictures which turned out to be illustrations for a story published in January 1883, called "Fairy Wishes, Nowadays" by S. A. Shields. Of course the pictures would be remembered by anyone, for they are by A. B. Frost. The "Peterkin Papers" were running in *St. Nicholas*, and so were such serial stories as J. T. Trowbridge's "Tinkham Brothers' Tide-Mill" and "His One Fault." Palmer Cox's "Brownies" were at their best. But if Frank Stockton was the pre-eminent author, the finest story in the world was "Davy and the Goblin," which gave me more pleasure than I have found in the Hundred Best Books or the Five Foot Shelf or the Amalgamated World's Classics. A member of a banking-firm has told me they had recently among their customers a certain Mr. Carryl; once or twice he had seen him in the offices,— a little, silvery-haired gentleman of distinguished appearance. Only when his death was announced in the papers did the banker learn that this was ever so much more than a mere banking customer; he was Charles E. Carryl! "Why didn't you tell me who he was?" he demanded of the other bankers. "Oh, I believe he *had* written some books, once," said they. *"Books!"* exclaimed my friend, "he wrote *'Davy and the Goblin'!"*

Mr. Carryl's only other books, so far as I am aware, are "The Admiral's Caravan," which includes the priceless poem about the camel, and a book of short stories for adults, "The River Syndicate." Mr. Reginald Birch made the pictures for "The Admiral's Caravan" as Mr. Bensell did for "Davy," so again we have these two admirable artists helping to enhance the work of one author. "Davy," in book form is dedicated to the author's little son, Guy Wetmore Carryl, later to become distinguished as a poet, inheriting his father's metrical ingenuity. It is a surprise to find how quickly the story came and went in *St. Nicholas;* the first chapters appeared in the number for December 1884, and the last of them in the following March. Between those months the Cockalorum arrived, perched upon Davy's hat, as Davy and the hat went whirling through space, softly murmured his beautiful name, and flapped heavily away. Davy fell through the barley-sugar sky-light and thereby enraged the Hole-keeper, who might easily be forgiven, since he was in danger of being boiled. Sham-Sham, the sole survivor of the famous Forty-Thieves appeared, and demonstrated his peculiar method of treating a pot full of boiling watches. The Cockalorum fell ill, to the alarm of his friends, and Sindbad recited "A capital ship for an ocean trip," a song which has since been trolled out by thousands of soloists and glee-clubs, without any notion of its origin. Ribsy, the cab-horse, gallops up, drawing the cab which was so strangely furnished with a bath-tub, whose faucets exuded nothing but dust and bits of gravel. Ribsy recites:

> As spry as a kid and as trim as a spider
>   Was I in the days of the Turnip-top Hunt,
> When I used to get rid of the weight of my rider
>   And canter contentedly in at the front.

By permission Houghton Mifflin Co.

From "Davy and the Goblin"

It made me a wreck with no hope of improvement,
   Too feeble to race with an invalid crab;
I'm wry in the neck with a rickety movement
   Peculiarly suited for driving a cab.

"And canter contentedly in at the front"—how does the famous *"Quadrupedante putrem"* line in Virgil excel that? Davy visits Robinson Crusoe and hears another famous poem, beginning: "The night was thick and hazy, When the 'Piccadilly Daisy.' " Other adventures follow, the Cockalorum recovers from his indisposition, and the believing voyage comes to an end.

As Charles E. Carryl's book was hardly inferior to those of his great predecessor, Lewis Carroll (he acknowledges his debt to "Alice in Wonderland") so we had in Mrs. Laura E. Richards a writer of nonsense verse and humorous poetry who does not suffer by comparison with Edward Lear. The longer poems of Lear, such as "The Owl and the Pussy-Cat," "The Dong with the Luminous Nose," "The Pelican Chorus" constitute the best work of this distinguished pioneer in nonsense writing. His limericks, about which a great deal of undiscriminating praise is uttered, are, with half a dozen exceptions, inferior in construction to those by some later writers. Lear's last line is a repetition, both of rhyme and idea, of his first line, and so he cannot equal for humorous effect the limericks in which the surprise is coincident with the end of the poem. The limerick is worthy of respect. Mr. Brander Matthews, in "A Study of Versification," declares that it "has the distinction of being the only form which is actually indigenous to English. . . . The limerick alone seems to have been born where the English tongue is spoken." And so it is worth remembering that although some of Lear's are unsurpassed as *nonsense* verses, they do not qualify as perfect limericks. To show what I mean, let me quote two examples, —one by Edward Lear, and one which is anonymous. Here is a typical one (not a *pure* nonsense verse) by Lear:

> There was an old man in a pew
> Whose waistcoat was spotted with blue;
> But he tore it in pieces
> To give to his nieces,
> That cheerful old man in a pew.

The anonymous example which follows, is not a nonsense verse at all; it neither employs nonsense words nor is the incident in any way impossible or even improbable. We have all known many young persons like Maud. But in construction, in keeping the climax for the last word of the stanza, it approaches perfection. Lear repeats the rhyme-word, "pew"; the anonymous writer introduces a fresh, although not a perfect, rhyme:

> There was a young lady named **Maud**,
> And she was a terrible fraud;
> To eat at the table
> She never was able,
> But out in the pantry—Oh, Lord!

But this arose from speaking of Mrs. Laura E. Richards, and her humorous poetry for children, which like all the really good work in this field, may be enjoyed by the children's parents without loss of self-respect. I do not seem to find Mrs. Richards' successor among the writers of today; perhaps I do not search carefully enough. Mr.

By permission Houghton Mifflin Co.

From "Davy and the Goblin"

Roosevelt refers to her verses about the Whale, "with a feather in his tail, who lived in the Greenland sea" and also to what he calls "the delightfully light-hearted 'Young Man from New Mexico, Who lost his Grandmother out in the snow.'" My book did not contain these. It is called "Sketches and Scraps" and I notice that it was given me at Christmas, 1884. The colored pictures are by Henry Richards, and few works of art are so familiar to me as every detail of these, from the heavily dyed beard on the servitor of Bobbily Boo, the king so free,* to the monocle in the eye of the Fourth Turk, who is coming out to battle with Ponsonby Perks.† But the longer ballads are the chief joys of Mrs. Richards' book. There is "The Seven Little Tigers and their Aged Cook."

> Seven little Tigers they sat them in a row,
> Their seven little dinners for to eat,
> And each of the troop had a little plate of soup,
> The effect of which was singularly neat.

The Tigers at their well ordered table, the blue china on the dresser, the portrait of the ancestor, and the armorial crests in the stained glass window, make up the picture which accompanies the opening stanza. The poem proceeds into deep shades of tragedy.

* He used to drink the Mango Tea
    Mango Tea and Coffee too,
  He drank them both till his nose turned blue.

† He fought with Turks,
  Performing many wonderful works.
  He killed over forty,
  High minded and haughty.
  And cut off their heads with smiles and smirks.

There was also the Frog, who lived in a bog, on the banks of Lake Okeefinokee, but the *chef-d'œuvre* is probably

> The tale of the little Cossack,
> Who lived by the river Don.
> He sat on a sea-green hassock,
> And his grandfather's name was John.
> His grandfather's name was John, my dears,
> And he lived upon bottled stout,
> And when he was found to be not at home,
> He was frequently found to be out.
>
> The tale of the little Cossack,
> He sat by the river side,
> And wept when he heard the people say
> That his hair was probably dyed,
> That his hair was probably dyed, my dears,
> And his teeth were undoubtedly sham,
> "If this be true," quoth the little Cossack,
> What a poor little thing I am!"
>
> The tale of the little Cossack,
> He sat by the river's brim,
> And he looked at the little fishes,
> And the fishes looked back at him,
> The fishes looked back at him, my dears,
> And winked at him, which was wuss,
> "If this be true, my friend," they said,
> "You'd better come down to us."

*   *   *   *   *   *
*   *   *   *   *   *

Other names of writers which return to me from these years are Mark Twain, whose two most famous stories, as well as that excellent, dramatic tale, "The Prince and the Pauper," were then easily obtainable with all the

THE SEVEN LITTLE TIGERS
AND THE AGED COOK.

Seven little Tigers they sat them in a row,
Their seven little dinners for to eat,
And each of the troop had a little plate of soup,
The effect of which was singularly neat.

original illustrations; Jules Verne; Louisa Alcott, whose "Jack and Jill" has left a dim recollection as a book of peculiar charm, although I cannot recall what that charm was; and of course, Lewis Carroll. Of *his* two most famous books it would be repetitious to speak; but the thought of his curious two-volume work detains me. I mean "Sylvie and Bruno." The illustrations by Harry Furniss are hardly less ingenious and interesting than the Tenniel pictures for the Alice books. Mr. Furniss's own volume of recollections furnishes some odd sidelights upon Lewis Carroll. I have the first part of "Sylvie and Bruno"; for the second, I must go to dealers in first editions, and to them I can only say, in the words of the Mad Hatter: "I'm a poor man, your Majesty." It is noticeable that the Hatter went down on one knee, as he said it, and that *he lost his bread-and-butter*,—token of what happens if you frequent dealers in first editions.

The publishers of "Sylvie and Bruno" issue it now only in a one volume edition; a condensed version for children. I would speak to them, harshly, about this, if it were not for (*a*) the fact that I have great respect for their taste in authors, and (*b*) it is possible that they know what they are about in this instance. Few would care for the complete work today; it is a strange mixture of juvenile fiction, religion for grown people, and a dozen other things. Yet, everything considered, a book to covet.

In the shelf where many of these books stand, I notice one other, stained with paste and rain-drops, and earth. It tells how to make a hundred un-useful and delightful things: "The American Boy's Handy Book," by Dan Beard. I sometimes see the author on the street, and long to stop him and tell him how much string, and gun-powder, and glue, and buckshot, and how many fish-hooks and eels' ears and other things I employed in trying to follow his recipes—and what a good time I had.

Boots for Horizontal Rain. By Harry Furniss in
"Sylvie and Bruno"

THE SEARCH FOR CURIOUS BOOKS, I

CHAPTER V

To discover one curious book requires long search, and great patience. How long it takes, I do not know; I have been hunting for years, and never yet— unaided—have I found one. The term curious, especially in the form Curiosa, is in bad repute. In book-sellers' catalogues it denotes a certain unchanging type of mild pornography,—just bad enough to invite a leer, and not actually bad enough to be prohibited. In short, bait for freshmen and sophomores. The most tiresome shelf in a book-shop is that row of red and white books which comprises the six or seven erotic classics of Italy and France. The most unimaginative type of book-seller is the one who always responds to a mention of Mark Twain by offering a copy of "1601." There are two humbugs created by this class of book: the man who pretends never to read nor enjoy any of them; and the man who repeats hypocrisies about "style" and "artistic achievement" and gives every reason but his true one for reading them. Book-sellers recognize from afar the "student," or "schol- arly" investigator, who is leading gradually up to a re- quest for some notorious book. Eugene Field, whose ex- cursions into this realm (in all shades, from pink to bright scarlet) are possibly not worth the whispering they have caused, wrote a good poem in the one called

"Boccaccio." Another honest reference to the subject is in Mr. Edwin Meade Robinson's excellent novel, "Enter Jerry." Best of all, in its frank and humorous admission of human weakness and natural curiosity about such writings, is John Hay's letter about Mark Twain's experiment in the vein of Rabelais. To pull a few proofs of the story, he writes in mock austerity, is highly attractive and of course highly immoral, "but if you take these proofs in spite of my prohibition, save me one."

But I have been led astray while pointing out that this chapter is not about "Curiosa." Instead, it is about those odd and unusual books which either deal with a strange subject, or which by their manner fall into a peculiar class of their own,—not infrequently the class of unintentional humor. Works on astrology or witchcraft, and the Seventeenth Century volumes on medicine, domestic remedies, and charms, are examples of the one kind; the Portuguese manual for conversation in our language, "English as She is Spoke," is one of the other kind.

To discover such a book is as hard today as to find a new island. There is a legend in one of Stevenson's stories about a party of wanderers who came upon a very old man shod with iron. He asked them whither they were going, and they answered: "To the Eternal City!" He looked upon them gravely. "I have sought it," he said, "over the most part of the world. Three such pairs as I now carry on my feet have I worn out upon this pilgrimage, and now the fourth is growing slender underneath my steps. And all this while I have not found the city."

I feel like this old man with the iron shoes. For four or five or six presidentiads—as Walt Whitman would say, in his simple and unaffected style—I have stood gaping at book-shelves in libraries. On stifling hot evenings in summer I have wandered through those glass and steel furnaces called book-stacks, or stood almost upon my head to peer into dark corners on the lower shelves of older, dustier, libraries and bookshops. "And all the while I have not found the city." Never have I scored off my own bat; the best of my luck has been to make discoveries at second hand, to find in some other man's book the record of what he had chanced upon. So, in a volume by Mr. Gosse, I think, I came upon his essay on Thomas Amory and was led thereby to read (or to read *in*) Amory's preposterous feat of unconscious humor: "The Life and Opinions of John Buncle, Esq." This Eighteenth Century novel is now so popular that a modern edition has been printed; anybody may read it, and wonder if Amory could have written in entire seriousness the adventures of his absurd hero who wandered about England and Ireland, marrying one after another seven young ladies of matchless beauty and profound learning. No odder book, says Mr. Gosse, was published in England throughout the long life of the author. "Amory was a fervid admirer of womankind, and he favored a rare type, the learned lady who bears her learning lightly and can discuss 'the quadrations of curvilinear spaces' without ceasing to be 'a bouncing, dear delightful girl' and adroit in the preparation of toast and chocolate." John Buncle, so unctuously named, mourned and married his seven wives with such machine-like regularity that the holiness of matrimony seems to disappear under his observances of it more completely than when the ceremony is quite disregarded by a hero of the tribe of Don Juan. His learned heroines were the first, perhaps, of a long line. The modest and elegant female (is her name Edna Earle?) in "St. Elmo" could discuss abstruse philosophy as easily as the different Mrs. Buncles could soar off into the higher mathematics. The type recurs. Mr. Robert Chambers invented one young heroine who conversed with the hero in Latin; while Miss Edna Ferber recently tried to make her readers believe in a flapper of seventeen who could command the vocabulary of a Ph.D. of Berlin or Vienna.

The shelf which holds the slang dictionaries is a happy hunting ground. The slang dictionary is, in one way of looking at it, a profanation, like a collection of dead butterflies. The life of these vivid words and phrases was on the lips of the people; it is terrible to have them pawed about by fussy lexicographers, to see them chloroformed, pinned, and spread out for display in the even columns of a printed book. He must have given a narcotic to his sense of the ridiculous who can set down in ink: *"Let 'er go, Gallegher!* **An** expression signifying a readiness to proceed." Every slang dictionary is, of course, out of date before the printers can finish it; many of them are full of the most absurd blunders and misconceptions. The most complete slang dictionary in

English is "Slang and Its Analogues, Past and Present," in which the original compiler, John S. Farmer, was joined after the second volume by W. E. Henley. This extraordinarily interesting work, which adds to the English synonyms others in French, German and Italian, is made remarkable by its extracts and examples quoted from all contributions to English letters, from Chaucer and earlier writers down to the newspapers of 1904, the date of the final volume.

As the compilers were thorough in their work, and as slang is the speech of the people, not the studied language of literature, some pages of the work are hardly for the *jeune fille.* A copy which I have seen contains a manuscript note saying—I know not on what authority—that after the second volume was printed, the printer refused to proceed with the work, asserting that his compositors' modesty was outraged and that they objected to putting it into type! This discovery of such squeamish printers recalls the peculiar crew of Captain Hook's pirate-ship in "Peter Pan"—especially the pirate who used to work at a sewing-machine, and cry because he had no mother.

Their evil geniuses constantly inspire Englishmen to write lexicons of American slang, or to include definitions of Americanisms in general works on slang. Francis Grose was probably the first to venture into these dangerous paths; his "Classical Dictionary of the Vulgar Tongue" appeared in 1785. He defined but few Americanisms, but the day when I found one of them remains in my mind like that on which Cortez stood silent on his peak in Darien. This is it:

> To Gouge. To squeeze out a man's eye with the thumb: a cruel practise used by the Bostonians in America.

The gem of such definitions, of course, is the famous entry under "Jag" in John S. Farmer's "Americanisms,— Old and New," published in London in 1889. Mr. Farmer starts well:

> Jag. In New England a parcel; bundle; or load. An old English provincialism which held ground colloquially across the Atlantic.

> Cleveland was forced up 7½ cents by the persistent bidding of one broker buying a heavy order. He occasionally caught a Jag of 2,000 or 3,000 shares, but kept on bidding as if Cleveland were the only thing dear to him on earth . . . *Missouri Republican* 1888.

But he continues:

> Jag is also a slang term for an umbrella, possibly from that article being so constantly carried.

And he proceeds to prove this by a quotation from the Albany *Journal*:

> He came in very late (after an unsuccessful effort to unlock the front door with his umbrella) through an unfastened coal-hole in the sidewalk. Coming to himself toward daylight, he found himself—spring overcoat, silk hat, Jag and all—stretched out in the bath-tub.

In justice to Mr. Farmer it should be said that he learned as he proceeded. His "Slang and its Analogues," of which the first volume was published in 1890, abandons the umbrella and defines "jag" briefly but correctly. This work shows a vast improvement in accuracy over the earlier one; I have not found in it any error in defining American slang.

As late as 1909 Mr. J. Redding Ware, author of "Passing English of the Victorian Era," essayed the definition of much American slang. His success may be explained by supposing that he had attended a college said to exist in Great Britain for the purpose of teaching ignorance about things American. We have a branch of it in America in which ignorance about England is inculcated. Mr. W. J. Ghent, in a review of the book, suggested that Mr. Ware lighted a lamp, retired into a closet, and evolved a meaning from his inner consciousness,—like the German scholar with the dromedary. How else, asked Mr. Ghent, could he have defined "stuck-up" as meaning "moneyless—very figurative expression derived from being 'stuck-up' by highwaymen," after which, this etymologist profoundly remarks, "You have no money left in your pocket."

Some other oddities of Mr. Ware's book were mentioned by Mr. Ghent. A chump (not exclusively an Americanism) is defined as "a youth (as a rule) who is in any way cheated of his money—especially by the so-called gentler sex." "Snakes" is given, in Anglo-American slang, as meaning "danger" so "snakes alive" (wholly American) is "worse than snakes." Naturally the latter is too horrible to consider. Why Mr. Ware should say that axe-grinders are "men who grumble, especially politically," is hard to understand, since he has given, directly above, the correct definition of "axe to grind."

A few more misunderstandings, not mentioned by Mr.

Ghent, occur in "Passing English." For example, Mr. Ware evidently knows nothing of the command to "dry up!" He is content to say that the phrase means "to cease because effete"—from mountain torrents which dry up in summer. "Foxes," he says, are "people of Maine— probably owing to the foxes which prevail there." He heard of an American oath which he calls "Gaul darned." (Obviously, a term applied to anything condemned in Gaul.) His book is strong on our oaths—"Jee," he declares, is "an oath-like expression. First syllable of Jerusalem. 'Jee! You don't dare to do it!'" (Both "Jee" and "Gaul-darned" give evidence that Mr. Ware learned his American oaths by ear.) "Red peppers," he suggests, is another American "form of swearing." "Jag" is again a stumbling-block. Mr. Ware finds it to be a Spanish-American-English phrase to express a "desire to use a knife against somebody—to jag him." "Wake-snakes" means "provoke to the uttermost." And to "Whoop up" is an Americanism signifying "to tune a musical instrument."

"Bull-doze" is defined as "political bullying." But the lexicographer is not content with this—he must quote an anecdote, " 'What do they mean by bull-dozing?' asked an inquisitive wife the other evening. 'I suppose they mean a bull that is half asleep.' And the injured one kept on with her sewing, but said nothing." This, writes Mr. Ware, "will show that even in the U. S. A. themselves, this term is not fully understood." "Dod-rottedest" is "an example of evasive swearing." That is very true, but a little disappointing. He defines "Dime museum" none too accurately, and adds the gratuitous remark that a dime is "the eighth of a dollar." But this is enough of Mr. Ware's curious conjectures, especially since his book, so far as it concerns Americanisms, has again been flayed in a recent authoritative work by an American writer, Mr. Gilbert Tucker's "American English."

The odd or curious book may turn up in the course of your daily work. You may find fun even in an index or a table of contents. A readable index denotes a good book. And that sounds like a quotation from the book I am thinking about—"Kentucky Superstitions" by D. L. Thomas and Lucy B. Thomas. It has a delightful index. And its collection of signs, omens, and beliefs about lost articles, marriage, death and burial, sneezes, cures and preventives, fire, dreams, moon and signs of the zodiac, luck at cards, witches and hoodoos, and many other matters, make it a handy book of reference in any family. Handy, that is, if the charms are good outside Kentucky. Some of them are a bit complicated—I am not sure that the reward is worth the trouble in this one: "After you have taken a newly made quilt from the frame, toss a cat into it to make the quilt puff out. The girl that the cat goes towards will be married first."

Is it an adequate repayment for walking twenty-one rails of a railroad track to find under the twenty-first a hair of the same color as that of your destined husband or wife? "Turkeys dance before rain," says the book. I wonder if it is so; I would like to see them. "There will be rain if mice cry loudly at night." Here is one with inter-state jurisdiction: "To kill a toad will cause rain." I can vouch for that absolutely; it was true in Massachusetts as far back as 1888. Nobody ever killed a toad then without at least a shower, within a week or two. Tom Sawyer never knew this one: "If you are troubled by witches, it is a good plan to sleep with a meal sifter over the face. When the witches come to worry you, they are compelled to pass back and forth through every mesh. By this time you will have had sufficient sleep and can get up."

One of the greatest discoveries was when Mr. Lucas's elderly hero walked into Bemerton's book-shop and bought, on chance, the fifty-fifth book from the first shelf on the left, as high as his heart. It was a "fat volume in a yellow paper cover, for which I had to pay two solid English pounds." There are thousands, millions of people—even book-dealers—who have never seen "A Chinese Biographical Dictionary" by Herbert A. Giles, published in Shanghai by Kelly & Walsh. Some folk have even been known to question its existence. In spite of them, however, it is a real and rather heavy book of over a thousand pages, containing biographical sketches of 2579 men and women who lived in China any time during the last three thousand years. The copy which I am fortunate enough to possess came with its yellow covers unspotted, wrapped in a Chinese newspaper, and smelling pleasantly of the aromatic and mysterious East. As it was printed in Holland, I suppose it has crossed two oceans. Mr. Lucas has quoted much from it, but the field is large, and the harvest so tempting that I can

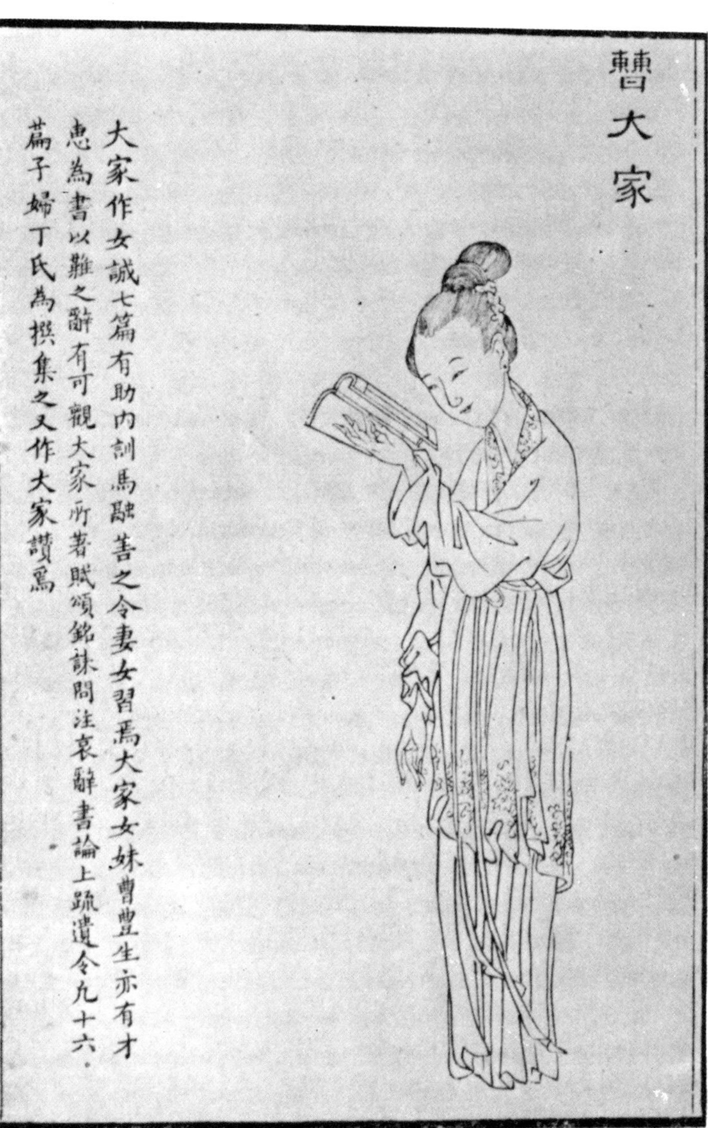

曹大家

大家作女誡七篇有助內訓馬融善之令妻女習焉大家女妹曹豐生亦有才
惠為書以難之辭有可觀大家所著賦頌銘誄問注哀辭書論上疏遺令九十六．
蕭子婦丁氏為撰集之又作大家讚焉

The Learned Pan Chao

(These Chinese portraits are from Wan Seaou Tang Hwa Chuen, published 1743*)*

gather in some more, and still not exhaust the possibilities of the book for its readers.

Its fascination is explained by a number of things. First, it is so long that you could not possibly read it through—even if you were silly enough to want to do so—in one, two, or three sittings. Like an immense jar of Canton preserved ginger, or a barrel of brown sugar in the pantry, there is always some there when you go back for more. Next, as you cannot, unless you are an erudite Sinologist, like the author, remember all these Chinese names, you are constantly forgetting your favorite characters, losing them for the time being, when you wish to read to your friends about them, and then having them turn up again, weeks later, when you are hunting for someone else—which is delicious. Third, Dr. Giles has put all together in one alphabet, the comic, tragic, pathetic, legendary, historical, mythical, comical-historical-pastoral personages of that strange and great country, paying no more and no less respect to a Chinese statesman of our own time who negotiated a treaty with Russia in 1893, than to an old man four thousand years ago who offended the gods by slaying two of their pet dragons, and was transported to the moon and set hoeing millet there forever and forever. It is as if somebody should write a biographical dictionary of England and America and combine in one list King Alfred, Mr. Hoover, Robin Hood, Mr. Henry Ford, Nell Gwynne, Thomas Jefferson, the Bailiff's Daughter of Islington, Jack Dempsey, Lord Beaconsfield, the Cheshire Cat, Mrs. Asquith, Babe Ruth, and the Old Man of Tarentum, who gnashed his false teeth till he bent 'em.

There is a strangely modern sound about the deeds of some of these Chinese worthies. Take Ou-yang Hsiu, who, although he died as long ago as 1072, "used his influence as Examiner to check the growing craze for eccentric writing and reasoning." He was the author of an elaborate treatise on the peony, was fond of wine and company, and described himself as "the drunken Governor." Liu Po-to, in the Third Century A.D., anticipated some of our contemporaries by being skilled in the preparation of a kind of whiskey. "It was so strong that a person who got drunk on it did not recover his senses for a month." Another, a statesman named Sang Wei-han, who died in 946, was high in favor with the Emperors of the later Chin dynasty, until, daring to suggest a regency while the Emperor was suffering from delirium tremens, he was dismissed to a provincial post. He was tremendously ugly, short of stature, and with a long beard. The very sight of him made people sweat even in mid-winter. But he used to stand before a mirror and say: "One foot of face is worth seven of body." Hsü Mo, who rose to be President of the Board of Works in 242, suffered from certain weaknesses— he was contemporary with Ts'ai Yung, whose fame as a wine-bibber, he rivalled, if not eclipsed. Evidently the Chinese government were trying experiments with prohibition, for "even when the use of liquor was altogether forbidden under the severest penalties, he was unable to resist the temptation of occasionally getting drunk." In the end, however, we learn that he was canonized. A good literary style has always been appreciated in state papers—especially in times of great danger: Han Yü,

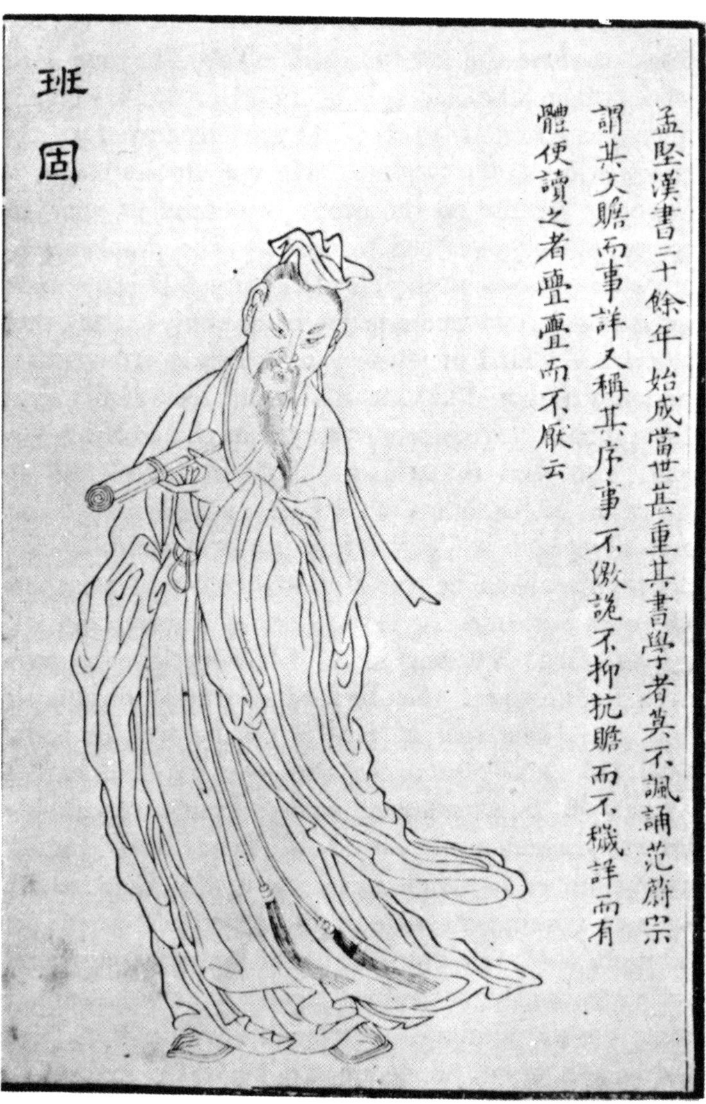

Pan Ku, impeached for altering the national history

who was born A.D. 768, found his neighborhood troubled by a huge crocodile, and the "denunciatory ultimatum" which he addressed to the monster and threw into the river, together with a pig and a goat, is still regarded as a model of Chinese composition.

Chang Yen-shang was a magistrate, who, on the occasion of an important criminal case, refused successive bribes of 30,000 and 50,000 strings of *cash*, but his virtue succumbed to an offer of 100,000 strings. He said that 100,000 strings would tempt even the gods, who would resent the refusal of such a bribe by a mere mortal. He died at the age of 61, and was canonized. Chao Tun, of the Seventh Century B.C., was the minister of a stern tyrant, Duke Ling of Chin. The Duke amused himself by shooting at his passing subjects from the top of a tower; also he put his cook to death for serving some badly prepared bears'-paws. Chao Tun remonstrated, and fell into disfavor. Ch'ên Ting fled from the offer of a cabinet position, and went with his wife into the country, where they occupied themselves in watering plants. Stoicism was his long suit, for on one occasion he went without food until he could neither see nor hear. His principles were so lofty, not to say impossible, that Mencius declared that a man would have to be an earthworm to carry them out.

Wang Ch'iao had no chariot nor horses, but used to come to court riding on a pair of wild ducks. One day he suddenly announced that God had sent for him, and after duly bathing, he lay down in a jade coffin and died. A learned and virtuous lady was Ts'ai Luan of the Fourth Century A.D. She studied the black art under Hsiu

Ying. She married a man named Wên Hsiao, and being very poor managed to earn money by making copies of a rhyming dictionary which she sold. I take it that her husband was a poor author and that she assisted him; their end was glorious, for after ten years they went up to Heaven together on a pair of white tigers.

Li Chin was a handsome and amiable young prince of the Eighth Century A.D. A hard drinker, he was enrolled as one of the Eight Immortals of the Wine Cup. (This was one of the two little groups founded by Li Po, the poet. The other was the Six Idlers of the Bamboo Brook. As they would say at Yale, Li Chin was not tapped for the Bamboo Brook.) Li Chin would swallow three large stoups of liquor before going to court, and yet a cart of barm, met in the road, would make his mouth water for more. He had some imitation gold and silver fishes and tortoises which he used to swim in an artificial pool of wine. He called himself "Prince Ferment" and also "President of the Board of Barm." Dr. Giles warns us that "his name has been wrongly given by some as Wang."

Contrast with this tippler the austere Yen Shu Tzŭ of the Fourth Century B.C. He was a man of the Lu State, who lived alone. One night a neighbor's house was blown down, and a girl took refuge with him. Accordingly he sat up until dawn, holding a lighted lamp in his hand!

Chiang Shih, who lived in the First Century A.D., was one of the twenty-four examples of filial piety, and his wife was one of his rivals in this virtue. She, because her mother-in-law preferred river water, used to trudge sev-

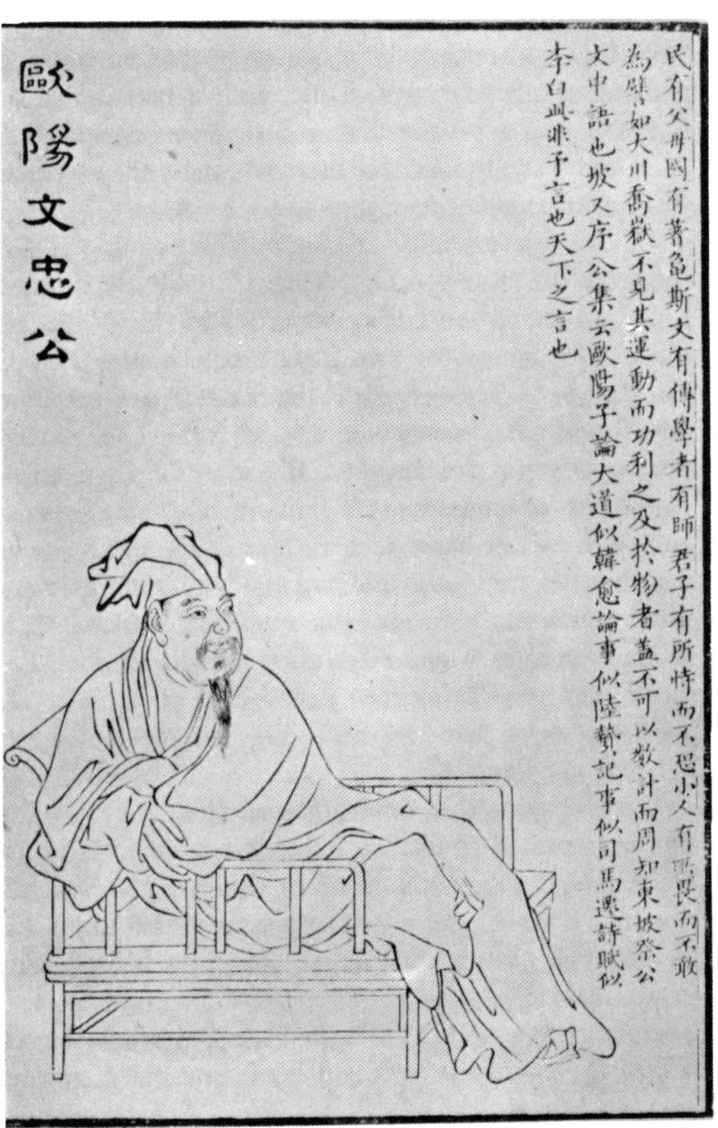

Ou-yang Hsiu, who opposed Modernism

eral miles every day to fetch it. The old lady was also very fond of minced fish, and an effort was made to provide her with it; the outcome of it all was that a spring burst forth near their dwelling with a flavor like river water. Daily it cast out on the bank two fine carp. One is surprised that the carp did not proceed to mince each other for her benefit; these examples of filial piety seem to have dealt in fish extensively. There is another of them—the name of the hero escapes me—who went to procure his stepmother, or mother-in-law, the fish that she craved, and on finding the pond frozen over, lay down naked on the ice, thawed out a hole with the heat of his body, and was rewarded with the conventional "two fine carp" which seem to have been the perpetual requirement of mothers-in-law. Another fish incident, by the way, concerns Chiang Tzŭ-ya, who flourished about the Eleventh Century B.C. He fished with a straight piece of iron instead of a hook, but the fish readily allowed themselves to be caught in order to satisfy the needs of this wise and virtuous old man.

Chu Hsi led an exemplary life—so remarkably that after death, to the embarrassment of his family, his coffin took up a position suspended in air, about three feet from the ground. Whereupon his son-in-law, falling upon his knees beside the bier, reminded the departed spirit of the great principles of which he had been such a brilliant exponent in life—and the coffin descended gently to the ground.

Li Ch'ung, of the Fourth Century A.D., used to attack with a sword anyone he found injuring the cypresses about his father's grave. He was secretary to Prime

Minister Wang Tao, and later to Ch'u P'ou, from whom he finally accepted a minor office, declaring that "a monkey in difficulties cannot stop to choose his favorite tree." The discovery of the elixir of life kept many of these personages busy; one of them poisoned himself and died from the effects of some of it. Liu An, however, actually discovered the precious fluid, drank, and rose up to Heaven in broad daylight. He dropped the vessel which had contained it into his court-yard as he rose, his dogs and poultry sipped the dregs, and immediately sailed up to Heaven after him.

There was a librarian named Wang Chi, of the Seventh Century A.D. He obtained a good post in the Imperial Library, but disliked the restraint and was always getting drunk. He retired, kept poultry, and grew millet— *from which he produced an ardent spirit!* He wrote a number of books on philosophy, many beautiful poems, and a short skit called "Note on Drunk-land."

The attractions of Tu I (of that prolific Fourth Century A.D.) are somewhat puzzling. He was, says Dr. Giles, a type of manly beauty. "He had a complexion like lard, and eyes like black lacquer."

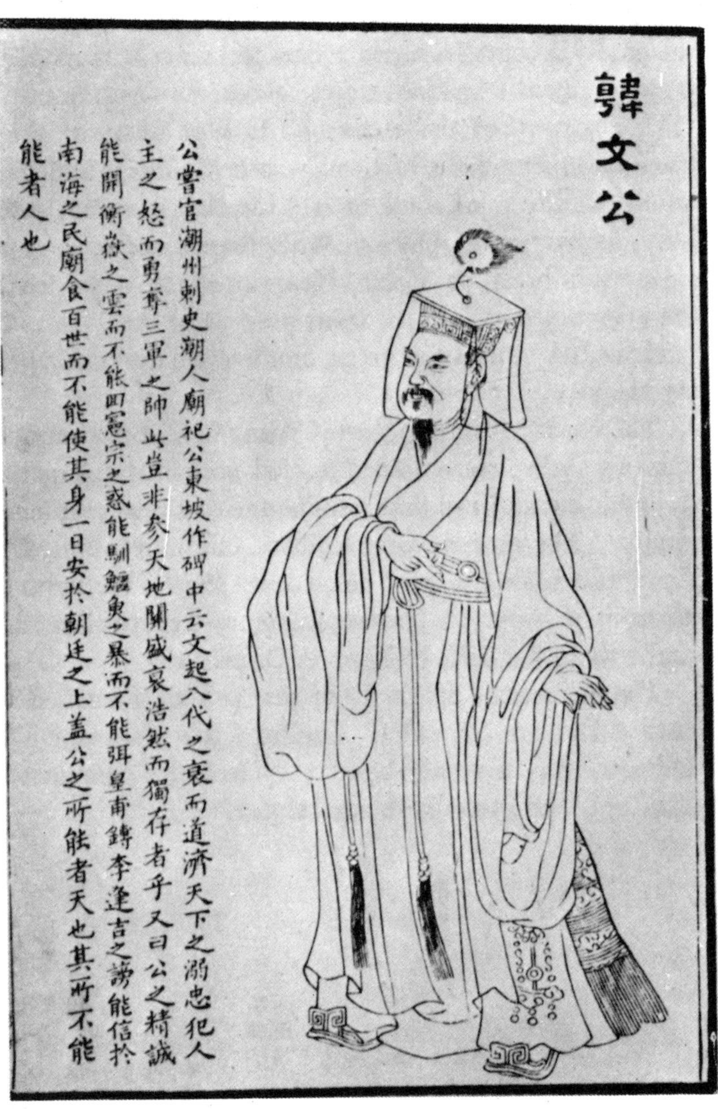

Han Yü, who wrote a Firm Note to a Crocodile, and won a
Diplomatic Victory

THE SEARCH FOR CURIOUS BOOKS, II

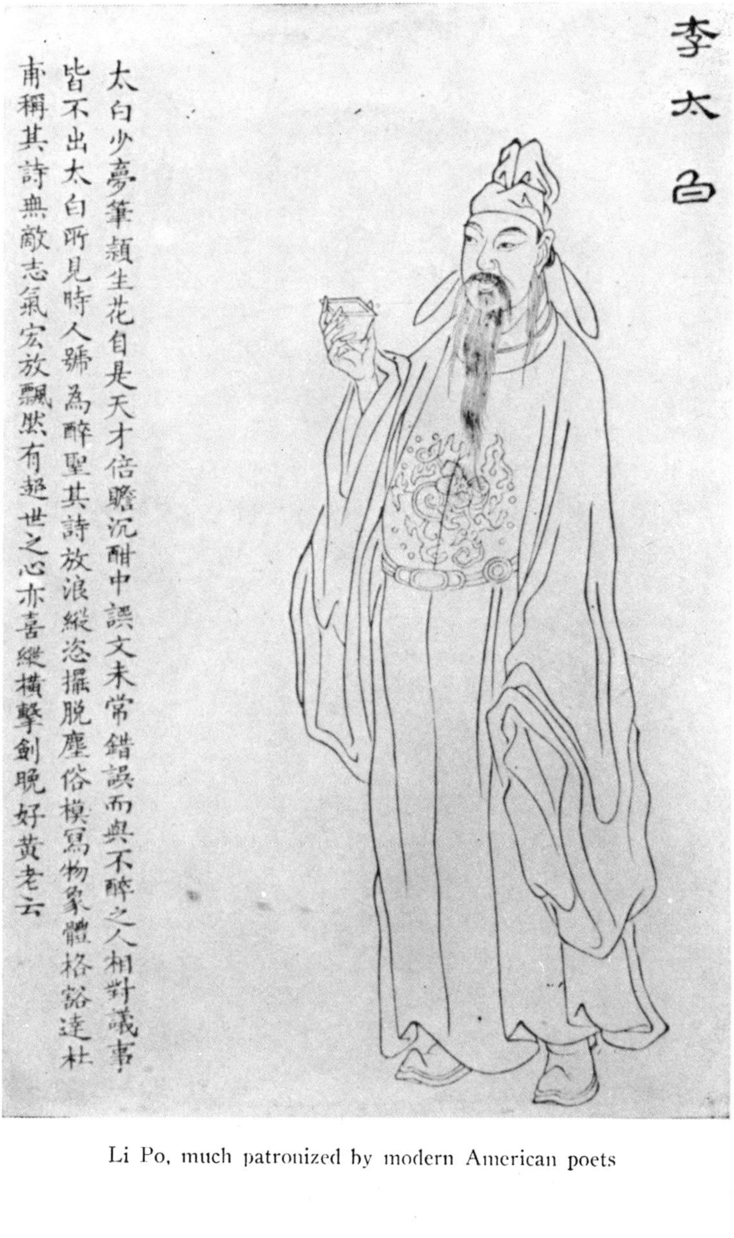

太白少夢筆頭生花自是天才倍贍沉酣中誤文未常錯誤而與不醉之人相對議事
皆不出太白所見時人號為醉聖其詩放浪縱恣擺脫塵俗模寫物象體格諮逸杜
甫稱其詩典敵志氣宏放飄然有超世之心亦喜縱橫擊劍晚好黃老云

Li Po, much patronized by modern American poets

CHAPTER VI

Book-collectors are divided into twelve or thirteen classes. There are also, in relation to books, certain sub-classes of human beings, who will some day be investigated and explained. These include the families or individuals who admit into their dwellings no other books except the Six Well-Bound Volumes permitted by interior decorators as the literary ration of a home. These are precisely placed on a table, between a pair of handsome "book-ends" (so called because it is an end to all normal use of books when you acquire them) and may be employed for pressing flowers, or as a place in which to conceal incriminating documents. Another mystic is the man or woman who never carries a book in the street unless it is wrapped in paper. Various explanations are given of this person's mental process. It has been urged that she is safeguarding the book against inclement weather. This fails, however, since the custom is observed on fair days as well as foul. There is a theory that the practice is part of that scheme of gentility which forbids anything unwrapped ever to be carried in the street,—any more than afternoon clothes may be worn after a certain hour, umbrellas go unfolded when not in use, or the human hands be seen in disgraceful nakedness outside the house. I think, however, that it is none of these. My belief is that the plan is to avoid the charge of being "literary," which may be preferred against the open and shameless conveyer of an uncovered book. The book concealed in paper may pass for a box of poker-chips, a case of cosmetics, an opium lay-out, or anything else which carries no social stigma. It is well to remember the point of view. A recently married pair at Niagara Falls on their honeymoon, were dressing for dinner in their hotel room. The husband, whose preparations were finished, sat down near a table and picked up a magazine —a copy of "Snappy Stories"—which had been left by a former visitor. The bride tip-toed across to him, looked over his shoulder to see what he was doing, and exclaimed: "My God, I've married a literary man!"

The book-collector is a man of wealth who assembles rare or unique books, early printed books, and first editions. There is some danger of being suspected of inverted snobbery, of the attitude of the fox toward the grapes, if you confess, as I do, that you regard his treasures calmly and without envy. His printed books of the Fifteenth Century are for the most part books which I cannot read; the perusal of medieval works of devotion is not one of my pleasures. As objects to be desired, for their own sake, without regard to reading, they excite me no more than old blue china. A Thackeray or Dickens novel in its "original parts," may thrill a collector, as one of the rarer triangular Cape of Good Hope stamps could once have thrilled me. Otherwise it is about as convenient as an automobile in its original parts.

There are books of which the first edition is, for one

which no one can conceive of who has not been in such a situation and felt that at any moment death might come. Presently a thought came into the bull's eye. I knew it! said I—if my nerve fails now, I am lost. Sure enough, it was just as I had dreaded, he started in to climb the tree—"

"What, the bull?"

"Of course—who else?"

"But a bull can't climb a tree."

"He can't, can't he? Since you know so much about it, did you ever see a bull try?"

"No! I never dreamt of such a thing."

"Well, then, what is the use of your talking that way, then? Because you never saw a thing done, is that any reason why it can't be done?"

"Well, all right—go on. What did you do?"

"The bull started up, and got along well for about ten feet, then slipped and slid back. I breathed easier. He tried it again—got

SUSPENDED OPERATIONS.

5†

"The buffalo climbing up the tree after Bemis."

reason or another, highly desirable, and others of which it is not desirable at all. So long as I can acquire for a dollar a good, fairly early edition of "Alice in Wonderland," in which the plates are not worn, and the picture of Alice and the Mouse on page 26 is sharp, with Alice's hair and the Mouse's whiskers clear-cut, I am content. If somebody else, who can do so, and wishes to do so, spends $250 for a first edition of it (which is really the second edition) with its covers liberally spotted with bread and butter,—why, he is an amusing creature and so is entitled to our gratitude. But that he is far removed from the Queen, in Frank Stockton's story, who collected button-holes, or Mark Twain's collector who specialized in buying *echoes*, is something which I leave to book-dealers to maintain, if they like.

To collect and worship beautiful book-bindings is to foster a charming art. It has much the same relation to books themselves as a collection of gems, or of specimens of carved jade. You will like your favorite modern authors in some "handsome" and "uniform" binding if you look upon books as part of your scheme of house-hold decoration. If the book in itself, in its associations with the days when you first loved it, in connection with what really made it a book—that is, the work of author and illustrator—if these things are important, you will prefer your old copy of "Roughing It," in its frayed, black cloth, and with the original pictures, especially the one of the buffalo climbing the tree after Bemis. And if somebody tells you that its market value is about a dollar and a quarter, you will not be troubled. There are men who talk as if authors were a kind of insect, allowed to exist only because they furnish those two great artists, the printer and the book-binder, material for their really important creations.

A collection of first editions may be extremely fascinating. It is lack of discrimination in selecting them, and the attempt constantly to add to the number of collectible authors which makes them absurd. The reader of books will always resent it if books which he could appreciate are gobbled up by someone who owns them merely to boast about them. The wealthy collector who can himself enjoy his books, and he who sooner or later makes his books available for others—whether the circle be large or small—these have never aroused any reasonable man's wrath.

Now, whether I long for "the books which never can be mine," or am sunk in indifference toward and ignorance about incunables and Elzevirs (which, as Andrew Lang says, are always regarded by novelists as the great prize of the collector) there is some form of book-hunting open to me, no matter how slight my learning nor how slender my pocket-book. Follow your fancy! Dr. Frank O'Brien's was for Beadle's Dime Novels, and he found himself the owner of a collection, interesting in itself, and, incidentally, worth many dollars. Mr. Franklin P. Adams writes that he has a collection of "bad poetry," which must be highly amusing, and moreover (to twang the financial string again) must have considerable value, if there are included the works of Mrs. Julia A. Moore, the Sweet Singer of Michigan.

Rearranging and rummaging in my book-case, not long ago, I assembled and gathered together upon one shelf a dozen or fifteen books which have been coming into my possession, one or two at a time, for the past three or four years. A friend of mine thought that he could do no better for my moral and spiritual benefit, than to send them to me. He seems to have believed that I was in need of that special kind of sacred counsel which was imparted to the young in the first half of the Nineteenth Century. They make a fine show on my shelf, now that I have them all together. Some of them have stamped leather or cloth bindings like the cases which used to enclose daguerreotypes,—the kind with the little brass hasp, and the red plush interior. Some of them, and this is appropriate to their contents, look like the ornamentation on a very swagger coffin. Here is "The Youth's Keepsake for 1846: A Christmas and New Year's Gift for Young People." The title-page is adorned with this rhyme:

> "Take it—'tis a gift of love,—
> That seeks thy good alone;
> Keep it for the giver's sake,
> And read it for thine own."

Among the others are:

The Girl's Week-Day Book. Published by The London Religious Tract Society. New York, 1837.

Sermons to Young Women. By James Fordyce, D.D. Boston, 1796.

Evenings' Entertainments, or, The Country Visit. Embellished with Fourteen Engravings. Prepared for the Presbyterian Board of Publication. Philadelphia, 1844.

An Analytical and Practical Grammar of the English Language. By Rev. Peter Bullions, D.D., Late Professor of Languages in the Albany Academy. New York, 1853.

Two Short Catechisms, Mutually Connected. By John Brown, Minister of the Gospel at Haddington, 1793.

The Jewel, or Token of Friendship. 1837.

The Ladies' Lexicon, and Parlour Companion. By William Grimshaw. Philadelphia, 1835.

The Pet Album. (For autographs.)

Woman's Worth; or Hints to Raise the Female Character. New York, 1854.

The Little Orator, or Primary School Speaker. By Charles Northend, A.M. New York, 1860.

The Hare-Bell; a Token of Friendship. Edited by Rev. C. W. Everest. "This little flower, that loves the lea, May well my simple emblem be." Hartford, 1844.

I keep the Rev. Peter Bullions's grammar in no spirit of derision. His name inspires awe, but his knowledge arouses my admiration and envy. Also, I observe that this was the *twenty-third* edition of his book. On the title-page of "The Girl's Week-Day Book" is traced in faint penciling the words *"Mon Cher Julie."* "The Pet Album" is mostly blank leaves,—rose colored or pale blue, or lemon, with a few engravings, "The Dead Bird," or "The Lost One Found." On one of the rose pages is written:

Way over here,
And out of sight,
I write my name,
Just out of spite.
Your loving
Cousin Lizzie.

Orange,
November 28, '73.

THE

GIRL'S WEEK-DAY BOOK.

PUBLISHED BY

THE LONDON RELIGIOUS TRACT SOCIETY.

REVISED.

"That our Daughters may be as corner-stones, polished after the
similitude of a palace."—Psalm cxliv. 12.

NEW YORK:

WILLIAM JACKSON, 33 CEDAR STREET.

M.DCC.XXXVII.

This *jeu d'esprit* impressed somebody named Annie so favorably that she repeated it on a blue page, on September 9, 1876, and even did it still again, two days later, on the next leaf,—ruling her lines carefully with pencil.

"The Hare-Bell" is the smallest and most chaste of them all. The gilded urn upon the cover, and the tiny mincing pages suggest pet lambs and pantalettes, forget-me-nots and maidenly reserve. The editor, the Rev. Mr. Everest, indulges his taste in an article from his own pen, called "The Old Man's Grave," which begins: "Buried in these painful reflections, I wandered on . . ." He soon comes to a cemetery, and says, what I can easily believe: "A churchyard seldom woos me in vain." Soon he is among the tombs, having a jolly good time of it, full of gloomy moralizings, which he desires to impart to his young readers. The frontispiece shows him, clad in a manner which would be considered depressing in an undertaker, and licking his chops over a coming burial party. "Soon the funeral procession appeared in sight, with slow and measured tread. I leaned against a tombstone and waited its approach."

These were the books which you were supposed to give to a girl on her seventeenth birthday.

"The Little Orator" contains poems which I had always believed to be more or less mythical, like "I'll Never Use Tobacco"—

> I'll never use tobacco, no,
>   It is a filthy weed:
> I'll never put it in my mouth,
>   Said little Robert Reid.

> Why, there was idle Jerry Jones,
>   As dirty as a pig,
> Who smoked when only ten years old,
>   And thought it made him big.

and the one about the robin who sang the "Temperance Song"—

> Teetotal—O, that's the first word of my lay:
> And then don't you see how I twitter away?

The Presbyterian "Evenings' Entertainments" tells about James and Thomas Jones, who as a reward for their obedience and diligence, were permitted to spend their summer holidays with their favorite Uncle John. Each evening they would gather on the veranda, where their uncle would deliver a twenty-page discourse upon the intelligence of ants, or the domestic virtues of the giraffe. Finally, on Sunday night they converse about keeping the Sabbath. Thomas relates an anecdote of his friend, Philip Oswald, who went sailing upon the Sabbath, and was drowned for his pains, while good Uncle John caps this by relating the untimely death of Philip's father, who, he is happy to say, died in a fever, because of *his* failure to observe the Sabbath. In fact the book is like the young lady's recitation in "Tom Sawyer" which wound up with "a sermon so destructive of all hope to non-Presbyterians that it took first prize."

Uplifting the youthful character, particularly the female character, which seems to be the conspicuous theme of this little collection, was assuredly the chief concern of the righteous authors of the 1830's and 1840's. Our grandmothers seem to have been docile girls! Did

THE

HARE-BELL;

A TOKEN OF FRIENDSHIP.

EDITED BY
REV. C. W. EVEREST.

" This little flower, that loves the lea,
May well my simple emblem be."

HARTFORD:
GURDON ROBINS, Jr.
1844.

Jolly Reading for Girls

they never revolt and wish for a less insistent harping upon female piety and meekness? Was there any relief for them if they did? It may be that there was: the writer of "Woman's Worth," hints darkly about "books of an opposite tendency, which, alas! are too much in vogue at the present day. . . ." There are works "of an infidel character . . ." and those "of an immoral" description. But he does not give their titles. This collection contains enough pious advice to make a school full of flappers today go into "shrieks of laughter," and then return to read books of a description which would make the hair of James Fordyce, D.D., the Rev. Peter Bullions, and the Rev. C. W. Everest curl with anguish.

Yet, I do not know. If the writers of that day, in their picture of model maidenhood, as they would have it, were no nearer the truth than the novelists of 1922 in showing the flapper, as they wish us to think she is, we may revise our views. Look at Charley, in Miss Edna Ferber's "The Girls." There are three Charlottes in the book, and the youngest, who represents the flapper—she is seventeen or eighteen,—is of course called Charley. "Charley," says the book, "speaks freely on subjects of which great-aunt Charlotte has never even heard. Words obstetrical, psychoanalytical, political, metaphysical, and eugenic, trip from Charley's tongue."

I wonder. I wonder if Miss Ferber really knows any flapper who is like that, or does she have to put her in the book because she had become a stock character, with which to flutter the provincial pigeon-coops. Mr. Scott Fitzgerald invented her, and now no writer of novels or short stories sits down to his typewriter without fishing up one or two from the depths of imagination. Just as no artist can take a stroll in the forest, along the side of a crystal brook, without happening upon a nymph or naiad about to plunge in, so is the novelist sure to know these slim, vivid young things—fine athletes (cf. Charley in "The Girls"), yet rather better informed in current literature and science than a university instructor. And all at seventeen or eighteen!

Actually, the flapper of today could not even pronounce all those jaw-crackers in Miss Ferber's second sentence. She is about as apt to turn red and uncomfortable at "words obstetrical" as her mother was at her age. She knows that psychoanalysis is something about dreams. She is stumped about politics if you are mean enough to ask her suddenly who is Speaker of the House, or how Senators are elected. Metaphysics is—er—oh, I think we take that up next semester. And eugenics means better babies—no it doesn't, it's purifying the milk supply, or else vaccination for typhoid, she's not sure which. With all respect to Miss Ferber's novel, I think that these wonderful flappers who haunt the fiction of the period of 1922 are going to be as grotesque to us in 1950 as the profound heroine of "St. Elmo," who at the age of sixteen discussed Stoic philosophy with the magnificent hero, or as the "dear, delightful, bouncing girls" who never flinched from conversing about the subtleties of astrophysics and Unitarianism, the while they prepared hot chocolate for John Buncle.

And as for her rattling game of tennis (Charley "packed a mean, back-handed wallop") there is invariably a cool woman of thirty-five in the same club who can make a

The Fate of Sabbath-Breakers

monkey out of her for three straight sets. Even her short skirts were old stuff. Take down your "Martian" by George Du Maurier, and look (page 139) at his picture of "Three Little Maids from School in 1853."

States of mind cannot be dated. Not many months ago I read a speech by an English bishop about the manners of today. He said that he tried not to be an old-fashioned parent, and yet when his daughter said to him, "I say, Old Egg, got any cigarettes?" he thought things had gone rather far. Yet at the same time, I doubt not, daughters could be found who spoke to their fathers in a style which would be approved by Dr. James Fordyce, whose "Sermons to Young Women" was published—my edition at least—in 1796.

To show that old-fashioned manners have not altogether decayed, let me quote from a guide to the art of correspondence which I read with some attention two or three years ago. Its date was about 1912 and the dates of the letters, a few of which I copied, show that the author writes practically within our own time. Here, for example, is his model for that most interesting of all letters—"From a gentleman to a lady offering her his hand":

Fairbury, Ill., May 6, 1899.

My Dear Miss Beane—It is now nearly a year and a half since I first had the great pleasure of being received at your home as a friend. During the greater part of that time there has been but one attraction, one strong hope, and that is your own personal attraction and the desire of winning your favor. Have I been successful? Has the deep faithful love that I felt for you met any response in your heart? I feel that my future happiness depends upon your answer. It is not the fleeting fancy of an hour, but the true abiding love that is founded upon respect and esteem, which has been for months my dearest life dream.

Your own maidenly dignity has kept your heart so securely hidden that I scarcely venture to hope I have a place there. I feel that I cannot endure suspense any longer, so write to win or lose all.

If you will be my wife, it will be my pride to shield you from all sorrow and give you all the happiness that a tender and loving husband can bestow upon the one he loves.

Hoping to hear from you soon, I am,

Devotedly yours,
C. H. RUMLEY.

MISS ALICE BEANE, Loda, Ill.

The gentle Alice kept Mr. Rumley on pins and needles for four days, and then from her maiden seclusion in Loda, Ill., sent him a wild outburst of passion, which the author of the book calls a "Favorable reply to preceding letter." Here it is:

Loda, Ill., May 10, 1899.

MY DEAR MR. RUMLEY—Your kind and manly letter surprises me of the fact that what I believed to be only a friendship consists of a stronger feeling. I see it would be a pain to me to lose your visits and your presence, and I am sure that such a love as you promise your wife would make me very happy. You see I answer you frankly, deeming it wrong to trifle with such affection as you offer me.

I have shown your letter to my parents and they say they will be pleased to have you visit us at your earliest convenience. Believe me to be,

Yours most affectionately,
ALICE BEANE.

MR. C. H. RUMLEY, Fairbury, Ill.

In order, however, that no maiden should be trapped into unfortunate marriages (or alliances, as the author would probably prefer to say), the book also gives the form for an "unfavorable reply to preceding letter." The author did not intend that the experience should be repeated of the American in France who was run away with by a horse, merely because he did not know the French for "Whoa!" Miss Beane is thoughtfully provided with a declination, couched in the most elegant phrases. I will omit it out of regard for the amorous Mr. C. H. Rumley (think of a hero known only as "C. H."!) and let his romance have a happy ending.

Upon the lover in the next drama, we need have no such mercy. There is something about his letter which makes me feel that he is planning by a second marriage to defraud his rightful heirs—the reference to his need of a "kindred spirit" is, I think, a sly dig at somebody. Besides, what can be said of a man who plans to ask a lady to forsake a place so beautifully named as Bellefontaine (even though local pronunciation degrades it into "Bell Fount'n") in order to dwell in Wapakoneta? Finally, there is more than a suspicion that the recipient of the proposal is well off—her very name suggests not only ample physical proportions but a comfortable bank account. Alfred is a giddy old rascal, and a fortune hunter into the bargain. Here is his letter, recommended by the author as the correct form, "to a widow from a widower":

Wapakoneta, O., Sept. 8, 1901.

My Dear Madam—I take this opportunity to lay open to you the present state of my feelings, having been so convinced of your good sense, and amiable disposition, that I feel assured that you will deal candidly with me in your reply. Like yourself, I have been deprived of the partner of my earlier life, and as I approach the middle state of existence, I feel more and more the want of some kindred spirit to share with me whatever years are reserved to me by Providence.

My fortune is such as to enable me to support a lady in the manner which I feel to be due to your accomplishments and position. I sincerely hope you will think carefully over my proposal. If you can make up your mind to share my fortune, I trust that no efforts will be wanting on my part to assure you of the happiness you so well deserve.

I need scarcely say that an early answer on the matter so much connected with my future happiness will be a great favor to

Your devoted admirer,
ALFRED REINHARDT.

MRS. MARTHA CAFFEY, Bellefontaine, O.

There is, as I intimated, a favorable reply to this letter, signed "Martha." But it does not ring true. Here is the genuine one. Note the stern reserve of the signature, not only the full name, but "Mrs." besides! Alfred is plainly told to keep his distance. Bellefontaine will see him no more, that is certain.

"Unfavorable reply to preceding letter":

Bellefontaine, O., Sept. 10, 1901.

DEAR SIR—You give me credit for a discernment I do not possess, for I declare to you I never suspected that there was anything beyond friendship in the sentiments you entertained toward me. I am sorry to find it otherwise, because it is out of my power to answer your question in the affirmative. I esteem you, but there I must pause. My heart is untouched. The probability is that I shall always remain a widow.

Wishing you with all my heart a more favorable response from some worthier object, I continue

Your sincere friend,
MRS. MARTHA CAFFEY.

MR. ALFRED REINHARDT, Wapakoneta, O.

The book has many other charming and useful models. Especially to be recommended is one "From a Gentleman Proposing the Day of Nuptials." There is a reply to it, from his prospective "life's partner." Another, in a minor key, is "From a Lady Confessing a Change of Feelings." There is also a brief note "To a Lady Complaining of Coldness" (doubtless from the janitor of her apartment house), while the "Letter to an Entire Stranger Seen at Church," and the "Reply" thereto are the central jewels of the whole cluster. This is a convenient model, and the frigid chastity of the "Entire Stranger's" reply makes Miss Felicia Hemans seem like burning Sappho by comparison.

The end is in gloom. Here is the correct letter to be sent "From a Gentleman to a Lady on Rejection of his Suit." Why the author has ironically adopted the name of Dr. Weir Mitchell's hero is hard to say. It should be observed that gentlemen suffering with rejection of the suit are not even allowed to use the formal and customary "Dear" or "My Dear" to precede the rejector's name. "Miss Murney" (a name doubtless selected for its hollow and dismal sound) is to be used in all its brevity. However this may be but a sign of misery from one who is an isolated lonely wanderer in Harrisburg, Pa. The sad epistle follows:

Harrisburg, Pa., Aug. 5, 1901.
Miss Murney—From the highest pinnacles of hope I have been sunk to the lowest depths of despair. Your rejection to my love has filled me with misery and wretchedness. I now feel an isolated lonely wanderer on the face of the earth, without one friendly ray of light to guide my way.

Still, whatever my fate or wherever I am, my one desire will be that you may be as happy as I have been made wretched.

From your admirer, though miserable,

HUGH WYNNE.

MISS ALBERTA MURNEY, Reading, Pa.

The mock-refinement of the uncultivated, and the affected roughness of the over-cultured produce strange effects in literature. It is not the New England poets who occasionally lapse into effeminacy of expression, but Walt Whitman. The big prize-fighter and the heroes of professional baseball turn up missing when the country goes to war, while the great prizes for gallantry go to a deacon of the church and to a studious, near-sighted lawyer. The "strong stuff" which has so occupied the writers of poetry and the drama for the last few years— is it loved by the people, or by a few under-nourished devotees? A teacher who had a small collection of books in her class room was surprised to see, one day, the tall and ungainly father of one of the pupils. He came in, said that he liked to read, and that he wished he might sit down and read for an hour or so. The pupils had gone, and there were various other persons in the room, which was sometimes used in place of a reading room. The man said that he liked "poetry," and so the teacher knew exactly what to give him. He had been, all his life, a cattle-man and cow-boy on the great plains. The teacher had learned, from the critics and the literary reviews, what these great, strong virile men preferred, so, not finding any of Carl Sandburg's poems, she gave him a volume of Whitman, and turned to the "Song of the Broad-Axe."

He did not seem to make much progress with it, and presently she saw him shuffling with the other books. Passing near him, as he sat reading, ten minutes later, she noticed that he had a copy of Tennyson. His head was bent low over the table, and he was perusing, apparently with the utmost delight, this:

> Airy, fairy Lilian,
> Flitting fairy Lilian,
> When I ask her if she love me,
> Claps her tiny hands above me,
> Laughing all she can;
> She'll not tell me if she love me,
> Cruel little Lilian.

There is a certain amount of pose in books about the sea, and in comments about them. A clever writer goes down to the wharf and smells tar or indigo or tapioca, or whatever it is that any good reporter on an assignment can always smell to please his editor, and comes back stuffed full of more romance than he or anybody else would experience in fourteen trips around the world. Such is literature. That the sailor-man with a seeing eye does behold signs and wonders I have no manner of doubt. Mr. Frank Bullen saw an extraordinary spectacle—a fight between an octopus and a whale—in the middle of a moonlit night. He ran below to tell the captain, so that

that mariner might enjoy it too. But he was rewarded by having a boot thrown at his head. I have talked with sailors and sea-captains who have had marvellous experiences—one of them had been in a collision on a calm sea in the Indian ocean, and had also been captured by the *Alabama*. And with others who could, for the life of them, after thirty years at sea, remember nothing more entrancing to discuss than the comparative prices of "corned shoulder" in Singapore, Colon, and Halifax.

In Captain Jacob Trent, master of the brig *Flying Scud*, you have a picture of a sea-captain. Stevenson has drawn it in "The Wrecker," that first-rate novel of the sea, of which three-fourths of the action is on land. Trent opened a bottle of Cape wine for his guests and discoursed of the one thing in his life which gave him pride: the pawn-shop, which, under the name of "bank," he had kept in Cardiff. "He had been forty years at sea, had five times suffered shipwreck, was once nine months the prisoner of a pepper rajah, and had seen service under fire in Chinese rivers; but the only thing he cared to talk about, the only thing of which he was vain or with which he thought it possible to interest a stranger, was his career as a money-lender in the slums of a sea-port town."

Almost always the romance of the sea ends at the water's edge. It is not what the sea contains, nor what it bears upon its surface, nor what takes place in ships upon it, that constitutes romance. It is what it causes men to imagine; the thoughts of what may lie below the blue rim. That is why W. W. Jacobs' stories are so good—they are coast-wise tales, or else yarns of men on shore talking about the sea. That is why Miss Fox-Smith's poems are excellent—she goes down to the docks and dreams dreams evoked by the names of the ships, and lets her fancy create the adventures they never have had. What are the best sea-stories? Men fight upon this theme until their eyelids will no longer wag. A year or two ago a great number of people were asked to write out their preferences and it finally worked down to me. I printed the names of my ten favorites, somewhere or other, and a man wrote in all the way from Hong Kong to say that (*a*) he had never heard of me in his life; and (*b*) that certain inclusions and omissions in my list gave him great anguish. And yet my list was not a bad one at all, although it maddened the man from Hong Kong.

And there is certainly good sea-adventuring. But not in the books which dwell long upon descriptions of storms and other kinds of weather. Mark Twain set an admirable precedent when he wrote at the beginning of one of his novels: "There is no weather in this book." One paragraph in "The Wrecker," one which it seems to me should attract to the novel anyone who has never enjoyed that story, is this:

> It is perhaps because I know the sequel, but I can never think upon this voyage without a profound sense of pity and mystery; of the ship (once the whim of a rich black-guard) faring with her battered fineries and upon her homely errand, across the plains of ocean, and past the gorgeous scenery of dawn and sunset; and the ship's company, so strangely assembled, so Britishly chuckle-headed, filling their days with chaff in place of conversation; no human book on

board with them except Hadden's Buckle, and not a creature fit either to read or to understand it; and the one mark of any civilized interest being when Carthew filled in his spare hours with the pencil and the brush: the whole unconscious crew of them posting in the meantime toward so tragic a disaster.

The guides to manners and to conversation have led me aside from the discussion of curious books. But in that category must certainly be included the missing and disappearing books, the books which you have read, but are now long lost, as well as the books which ought to have been written, but have somehow been neglected. There is an alluring description of one of the disappearing books in Mr. Maurice Baring's "The Puppet Show of Memory"—an informal autobiography well worth reading on its own account. Mr. Baring read this book when a boy; he remembers where he read it, and how he got it, he recalls the picture on the cover, and that the book "was called 'The Siege of Castle Something' and it was by—that is the question—who was it by?" It describes the adventures of a peculiar family who were besieged by their creditors; the humorous devices of the creditors to get at the family, and the extremely romantic and ingenious devices of the family to avoid being surprised. Once Mr. Baring met a man who was reported to have read everything; he described his lost book and the man—who was also a great traveller—instantly declared that he, too, had read and enjoyed the book. But neither could he remember the author, nor give any aid in tracking the book.

One of the most popular books in my first decade was a bulky pink pamphlet, the advertising catalogue of a certain firm. I wonder if it is still published. In it were set forth the attractive apparatuses by which you could make yourself beloved in any gathering: by locking firmly together two bashful persons (bachelor and spinster preferred) with a gutta-percha "finger-trap"; by presenting some dignified gentleman with a "trick cigar," which would "explode with a red light, killing the smoker and amusing the spectators"; by distributing whistles, recommended as "sending the girls into fits and driving the old folks crazy"; by wearing a boutonnière which might be made to squirt a thin stream of some deadly fluid into the eye of anybody who came near it. These amiable tricks were supposed to provide the utmost in refined entertainment, and to represent a nice taste in humor. The pamphlet which offered them for sale was adored by all my contemporaries, but liable to confiscation by parents and elders, who simply did not know a joke when they saw one. One of its treasures was a "fire-eating outfit." We used to look at that and dream of the day when we, like the man in the illustration, might stand clad in an evening suit, our faces adorned with the invariable moustache and imperial of the true fire-eater, and puff out smoke and flames, to the consternation of groups of little girls and boys in their best clothes. I knew one boy who tried it—and he is still alive.

An admirable book, which seems never to have been written, is a volume of essays on outdoor sports, treated strictly from the view-point of the amateur. You will say, immediately, that there are many such books, and many such essays. But it is not really so. The difficulty comes over the definition of the word "amateur." The original meaning of "lover" has, practically, been lost for ages, and its secondary meaning of "non-professional" has been allowed to usurp too much importance. Except in wrangles among colleges the distinction between the amateur and the professional is of little interest to any-one. The really important significance of the word lies in its connotation of lack of skill in this or that game or sport. And it is seldom so used—sincerely.

Therein lies the trouble. There is no end of books on angling, on golf, on tennis, all purporting to be by "An Amateur." It is the sheerest affectation. You can-not read one of them for half an hour without discovering that this self-styled amateur, this gentleman of violet-like modesty, is a wizard at his special game. Only the fact that he does not take money for it distinguishes him from the out and out professional. And what do you care about that when you are reading his book? Indeed, there would be less exasperation in a book by a profes-sional. You do not object if *he* outdistances you hope-lessly. But this person who hypocritically calls himself an amateur, and then proves inside twenty-five pages, to have performed the most astonishing feats—he plunges you into a fit of depression from which you may well be hours in emerging.

No; our book of athletic essays must be by undoubted amateurs. More than that, they must belong to the duffer class. Here again is a relative term—let it be understood if the subject is golf, that they shall be duffers not only in the presence of the lords of the game, but duffers anywhere, duffers amongst the humble and the lowly. In tennis, it is better that they should never get beyond the second, or perhaps the third, round of a tournament. The yachtsman whose view is most to be desired is the one who tends the sheet, perhaps—never the one who comes to the wheel in a pinch. And so on through the sports.

From these men, it is my contention, we should get new and refreshing work. They know the full joy of the game—and the full sorrow—and no more. Nothing of the mathematics of sport has corroded their souls—they do not bicker, overmuch, whether they took six or seven strokes at the fifth hole, but are content to cover the tragedy with a decent silence.

Not that they are without a respectable desire to win, if the sport is one involving contest. We want nothing mawkish in the book. Of course, they hope to beat their opponents. But this desire must be nicely measured; winning is an important ingredient in their pleasure, but not the whole of it. The contest is something, the surroundings are much. The man to whom it is of no importance whether the tennis court is in the midst of green meadows or between brick walls in a city, and the man who leaps upon the court with an iron face and wields his racquet like an axe, will not be asked to contribute.

Tennis,* golf, angling, and yachting—these have al-

* Perhaps the essay on tennis has been written, and that on swimming too: in Mr. A. S. Pier's "The Young in Heart." But Mr. Pier is not a duffer in tennis; I think he has played in tournaments with the great.

ready been named as subjects for the essays. To them should be added riding, motoring, with possibly an historical note on bicycling, mountain-climbing, plain walking, camping—with an excursus on camp cookery, canoeing, and swimming, next to the best of all. (Tennis is first.)

One section might be devoted to croquet, provided that emphasis was placed on the peculiarly disagreeable dispositions of all persons who are expert in that game, or who even tolerate it.

This should be a soothing book, a book for summer days, one to be carried in a canoe, and read on quiet streams. It should suggest the click of golf-balls, the smell of spring and autumn fires, and lengthening shadows upon the court. There should be a little of the heat of contest in it, but almost none of the wrath. The swimming should not be a mile race at top speed, but rather it should describe floating lazily upon one's back, hung between earth and sky, watching the clouds, surely the position in which man shakes off more of the bodily limitations—but the swimming is to be described by someone else.

"Let me tell you a secret," said Bunthorne to Patience. "I am not as bilious as I look. . . . There is more innocent fun within me than a casual spectator would imagine." This may be applied to the book of information. There is a literary critic who confesses to a weakness for Whitaker's Almanack, and another who admits that if he once pauses for a moment over the Dictionary of National Biography, he does not return to earth for hours. There is even a certain amount of innocent fun in an index. Not alone the deliberately humorous indexes —of which the great examples are in "The Biglow Papers," some of Holmes's works, like "The Poet at the Breakfast Table", and in Lewis Carroll's "Sylvie and Bruno." I mean the perfectly honest, sober index, like that in "The Anatomy of Melancholy" and best of all in Mr. Wheatley's edition of Pepys' Diary. That is the king-pin of all indexes. One man appears in it only to be described as "a little fuddled." Surely it is an awesome thing, and one almost sufficient to make us resolve to drink no more strong waters, to read of this man, doubtless a worthy Christian, of long life and good repute, but now, three centuries after he has gone to his rest, we can know absolutely nothing about him, except that on one occasion he was "a little fuddled"! And here are the entries in this wondrous index under the head "Periwig."

Periwig, Pepys wears one, iii, 109, 305; Pepys puts off the wearing of one for a while, iii, 248; one bought by Pepys, iii, 303; he buys a case for it, iii, 307; Pepys so altered by it that the Duke of York did not know him, iii, 312; Pepys has a second made from his own hair, iii, 319, 320; he sends one to the barber to be cleansed of its nits, iv, 178; he buys two more, vi, 232; Pepys agrees with the barber to keep his in order, viii, 31; his, set on fire, viii, 111; King and Duke of York first wear periwigs, iv, 40; danger of wearing periwigs during the Plague, v, 60; Ladies of Honor in, v, 305; periwig shops, iii, 109, 295, 306; vi, 397; viii, 127.

All the members of the tribe of "Who's Who" have furnished entertainment to many. They took their cue from the English annual, which has celebrated more than seventy birthdays, and gleams from its shelf, fat, red and prosperous, with its thirty thousand biographies.

An official whose last name is Abbas (his others are Kuli Khan) leads the procession, which winds through thousands of pages to the Rev. Mr. Zwemer who thus has the honor of bringing up the rearguard in both this and the American "Who's Who." I should not care to be Mr. Zwemer on pay-day (army style) in Who's Who land. The most modest of all the thirty thousand famous personages, if briefness of biography is any test, is the Earl of Burlington with only the one or two lines of print, which he furnishes about himself. He gives neither his academic honors, his medals nor rewards. He is silent as to his clubs, his town and country houses, his telephone and motor-car numbers. Whether he was mentioned in despatches in the South African War, or won the D.S.O. in the Great War; what are his politics, his religion, or what the name of his heir, the reader learns not. His recreations (that famous point of interest in this book) we may imagine, since the noble Earl has had only four birthdays.

John William Rivallon de la Poer writes himself down as Lord le Power and Coroghmore, Count of the Papal States, but admits that the Barony is "under attaint on account of the rebellion of 1688." They have long memories, they feed fat their ancient grudges in these old countries; an American would think that they might let by-gones be by-gones and give Lord le Power his Barony again.

The recreations and amusements of the English Who's Whosiers are always pleasing. There is the usual range. The Hon. and Rev. James Black Ronald likes "cycling, walking, reading, writing and smoking." Ah, me, I was a pale, young curate then! But Major General Sir Archibald Cameron Macdonell is the very pattern of a modern Major General—he "goes in a great deal for riding and coursing wolves." Mr. Bernard Shaw still says that his recreations are "anything except sport." For exercise, however, swimming, walking, and public speaking. Messrs. H. G. Wells and G. K. Chesterton refuse to describe their recreations. They may all have their fame and their literary prestige; let the Hon. and Rev. Mr. Ronald pace sedately his parish, and let Major General Sir Archibald gallop after his Canadian wolves—yes, and ride them, if he will. I would not exchange with any of them. I envy not Mr. Shaw his royalties nor the Major General his admirable war record. My hero of the whole long gallery of living pictures is a shyer, more reticent figure. I imagine, although I do not know, that his clothes are beautiful. My modest ambition would be satisfied if I could exchange places with him—the Nawab Bahadur of Murshedabad. He is, as he says, "the 38th in descent from the Prophet of Arabia." And his recreations he describes in simple, manly fashion— "an athlete, keen at all kinds of sports; an excellent horseman; a brilliant polo-player, an excellent shot, and an A-one billiard-player."

THE BIRD

CHAPTER VII

THE BIRD

He was a subject of controversy as soon as he entered the library. The sailor who brought him appeared at my office, and said: "I've got him down here, but they won't let me bring him in, so I've checked him."

This gave me no great amount of information, so I sat still and stared. I was not sure whether a prisoner from an enemy submarine had been brought for my inspection, or if the sailor had arrived with some eccentric uncle who absolutely refused to stop smoking his pipe.* My office is in a rather cosy little library about the size of a royal palace. In that never correctly quoted saying of Kipling, it is asserted there are three great doors in the world, where, if you stand long enough, you shall meet anyone you wish. These are the head of the Suez Canal, Charing Cross Station, and the Nyanza Docks. In the days when the sailor paid me this call, we had come to believe that there was another place to be added to this list: the corner of Forty-second Street and Fifth Avenue. Presidents of the United States used to like to wave their shiny hats and review parades from our terrace; while inside the building we were fairly accustomed to the presence of Cardinals, Princes, and Field Marshals. One of my colleagues, who was asked one day where his small son had gone, replied vaguely: "I don't know; the

* A slavish follower, perhaps, of Mr. Christopher Morley.

last time I saw him he was in the children's reading room, talking to the Queen of Belgium."

All this gave the guards and the police some anxiety, and produced a little spirit of formality at the front door. This time the difficulty centered about a youthful West Indian parrot, about ten inches tall in his stocking feet. He, the party of the first part (hereinafter referred to as *Peter*) had arrived—in his travelling case—carried by the sailor aforesaid. The sailor was the commander of U.S.S. *Kennebec*, just in port after a year or two in the waters about Hayti and Santo Domingo, and as I went with him down to the front door, I thought how

> I should like to rise and go
> Where the golden apples grow—
> Where beneath another sky
> *Parrot* islands anchored lie.

The italics are mine. The officer at the door had been about to admit Peter without question. Peter was securely confined, the sailor wore the attractive summer uniform of the American Navy, set off tastefully about the shoulders with stripes of gold braid—the two seemed entitled to a safe conduct, if not considerable respect. But another guard raised the point whether parrots were allowed in the library. Peter was halted; a copy of the rules hunted up. Dogs, it seems, are expressly forbidden. On parrots the rules are silent. Objections seemed to be removed and the party again started upstairs for my office. But they were halted once more.

"Look here. Rule 5 says: 'Loud and unnecessary conversation is forbidden in the Reading Rooms.' Are you prepared to guarantee that that parrot will refrain from loud and unnecessary conversation?"

No. That could not be promised. And so as a measure of compromise, Peter was checked in the coat-room, while the sailor went to find me. I was brought down and presented. Peter maintained an air of aloofness. Even when told my name, and that he was thenceforth a member of my family, his was the attitude of W. S. Gilbert when informed that an International Exposition was to be held in Omaha. He received the news "with a calmness bordering upon complete indifference."

The ship's carpenter who had made Peter's travelling case worked with durability in mind, rather than æsthetic charm. He had sawn out and nailed together some boards which were stout enough to detain a particularly muscular emu. These were painted battleship gray, and on two sides of the box, where square openings had been made, wire net, ostrich-strong, was nailed. I think it was anti-U-boat net. Inside, on a stout perch, sat Peter.* There was a look in his eye which made me think of him as a confirmed landsman, who had been tossing about for ten days at sea, had finally been brought ashore, told that this was North America, and how did he like it?

Many months have gone by since that day, and I know Peter's moods and whims, his facial expressions and his language, spoken and unspoken, far better than I did then. I know what was the matter with him. He

* Mr. Don Marquis introduces a parrot named Peter in his play, "The Old Soak," and mentioned him earlier in *The Sun Dial*. To avoid suspicion of plagiarism I must say that the Peter of this essay was named in 1919, and is not, like Mr. Marquis's Peter, the creation of genius. He is an act of God, and liveth today.

had been on Government rations. He is an ex-service man, and I sympathize with him. For as soon as we got him home, and took him out of the box, we hunted up a banana (which we fancied might remind him of his lost home in Santo Domingo) and offered him a bit of it. Never have I seen determination and complete satisfaction expressed so promptly. He reached out for it, and took it in, as only Mr. Bryan could accept a nomination for the Presidency. He seemed to say: "Well, you've been a long while about it, but here it is at last."

And, holding the banana in one hand, balancing himself nicely on one leg, he commenced to eat it with gratified chuckles. Once, in a restaurant, I saw Diamond Jim Brady eating an elaborate dish, which the chef had spent an hour preparing. He made similar, pleased, little noises.

The *Kennebec* brought twenty-two parrots on that trip. When the crew learned that the ship had orders for home, they asked permission to bring parrots aboard. Hitherto they had been forbidden. Twenty-four hours before sailing, however, the prohibition was lifted, and parrot permits were issued. The boys of that West Indian town were notified and many a parrot home had cause to mourn a kidnapped son or daughter. The captives sat on deck, complained about the food, and squawked at each other. One, desperate about his abduction, flew into the air, and was reported lost at sea. The others arrived without casualty.

Peter's appearance is youthful; his colors are gay, and might be considered gaudy if they were not so well selected, and so tastefully arranged. In one respect only does his origin appear. Those antiquated looking feet, those aged claws, seem to hark back to a long buried past, and keep the secrets of the tomb about them, as, according to Walter Pater, Mona Lisa's smile recalled dim centuries when the world was young. By his decrepit steps upon those old claws, you are reminded of his ancestors of long ago, of his forefathers who chattered and screamed in the courts of Montezuma; who perched upon the slim, brown fingers of queens in ancient India; who, sedately mummified, accompanied the Kings of Egypt in their graves.

Otherwise there is nothing at all sepulchral about him. His feathers, as the light strikes them, vary from an apple-green to the deeper shades of the emerald and the peacock. The under feathers of his wings— when he spreads them, awfully, in flight—are navy blue. He has little rose-colored breeches, like a Zouave, and when, to express his gratitude, he spreads his coat-tails fan-wise, he displays a brilliant patch of scarlet. I know that this is a sign of gratitude, because in the Tailor Bird's Song, in the story of "Rikki Tikki Tavi," Darzee says:

> Give him the thanks of the birds,
> Bowing with tail-feathers spread,
> Praise him in nightingale words—
> Nay, I will praise him instead . . .

When he turns his back upon me, and bends his head to examine, more carefully, his cup of sunflower seeds, he looks (except for the green color of his coat) exactly like old Deacon Pettingill, as he used to walk of a Sunday up the main aisle of the First Unitarian Church, with the offering. But when he ruffles his feathers, draws up his shoulders in the manner of Napoleon the Great, shows me in profile his terrible beak, and glares at some distant object, I am forced to believe that he has seen, as I did once, Saint Gaudens' majestic American eagle upon the ten dollar gold-piece, and is doing his best to look like that. And when, in less war-like moments, he snuggles down in my lap, and chuckles and sniffles and whimpers and croons, while I tickle the small of his back, it seems to me that he has modelled himself and his conduct upon a fussy Plymouth Rock hen in the brooding season.

Never, until it was demonstrated, would I have believed that a bird of Peter's intense and tropical disposition would care to spend the evening—more than that, insist upon spending the evening, lying in an absurd position in my lap, asleep, with his head tucked under my coat. Intimate acquaintance with Peter has its price; of many visitors he disapproves altogether, and signifies this by biting *me*. I have shed no small amount of blood in learning that he does not care to have every caller approach too near.

There is the usual problem of how much he understands of what is being said in his presence. One stormy night in the winter we were reading aloud from Cable's "Strange True Stories of Louisiana"—something about an old ghost-haunted house in New Orleans. Peter sat upon the top of his cage, giving profound attention, and clasping the side of his face with one claw, like the Dodo, in "Alice." Suddenly, the storm had its effect upon the wires outside: the electric lights flickered, dimmed, came up again, and then faded into complete darkness.

"Now," apparently thought Peter, "is my time to give them a thrill!" And just before the room became entirely dark he uttered a terrible war-whoop, spread his wings and sailed straight at me, looking as large and terrific as a condor in its flight. He soared over my head and lighted, not upon a pallid bust of Pallas, but upon a portrait of Edgar Allan Poe which hung on one side of a book-case. There was a great hurroosh, a wild flapping and a crash, as Peter and Edgar Allan came down to the floor together—the picture in a state of ruin in which it remains today—"to witness if I lie."

Peter might be trying to qualify himself as an after-dinner speaker. For he manages to talk, or seem to talk, longer, and to say less than anyone, except an orator speaking about education, or world-peace, or any other of the great, vague topics. His actual powers of discourse, of imparting ideas, are limited. But his apparent flow of talk is like the water coming down at Lodore. Left alone in a room, he begins a low murmur of what he calls conversation. I translate:

Well, they've done it again—yes, they have—gone off and left me here in the window—no fresh seed, no apple, ain't had a thing since breakfast, and now they go into another room and leave me here to entertain myself—pretty fine sort of treatment I call it, why, dod-gast 'em all, what do they think I'll stand for? Hey, tell me that, will you? I've half a mind to give a hell of a yell—that would fetch 'em all right. All these old seeds too; nothin' in 'em, got all the good out of 'em long ago. Well, I'll heave a fist full onto the floor—that'll make 'em sorry they used me so. I'll say so! I'll say it will! Now, I'll go down stairs, down in the bottom of the cage, and scratch some sand overboard— that always makes 'em pretty peevish! Here goes, then, head down, lower yourself off your perch head first, Father used to say, and I guess the old boy knew the proper way, if anyone did. . . . Easy now, e-a-s-y, and s-l-o-w does it, no use rushin'. Other leg, now, one at a time—safety first, old top! There we are. And while I'm here it wouldn't do no harm to say *I've got a hair cut! Got a hair cut!* Yes, I have. Now let's see what next? Oh yes, scratch a little sand overboard. There's a sunflower seed—must have missed that at breakfast. Well, we'll take care of that all right, um-m-m, thirty-two chews to each mouthful; Fletcherize, hey, what? That's why we live to be a hundred. By the way, guess I'll go up on that perch again, perhaps I can get him to come and scratchem head! *Scratchem head!* Here goes now. First I stand on my head—like the White Knight getting over a gate—then reach up with my hind leg, and grab the perch with that. E-a-s-y now, g-o s-l-o-w, now, g-o s-l-o-w, only fool Americans kill themselves rushin'. Here we are again, now let's see if it will work. First, I'll ruffle up all the feathers on my head and neck, bend over my head, and close one eye, with an especially imbecile look, then grab the side of my face with one claw. He never can resist that. He'll scratch my head for me, when he sees me, after I strike the pose. Now, all ready, camera! *Scratchem head! Scratchem head!* There, he's comin'. Hold it! As you were! Now, in a wheezy tone: *Scratchem head!* Here he comes! What did I tell yer?

I have been on amiable terms, at one time or another, with two dogs and a horse; have been rather friendly with five or six fish, some turtles, with one rabbit (white), one mouse (white), an alligator, four lizards, a pigeon, some small snakes, a crow, two ducks, some hens, two canaries and a toad. I have had more than a passing acquaintance with a toucan, a kiwi, who was losing his eyesight, a chipmunk, three extraordinary otters (the best of all!), a marabou stork of polygamous habits and extremely disreputable countenance, a pelican, and a coypu

—who for fastidiousness about his personal appearance made Beau Brummel seem a sloven. In no one of these have I failed to discover, even after the shortest acquaintance, a distinct and a pleasing personality. He who fancies that one red hen is exactly like another red hen only displays his own pitiful ignorance. And it is through individuality, as I once heard a wise man say (his name was Josiah Royce), that we win immortality. Or, as it goes, in some verses by Walter Savage Landor:

> Life (priest and poet say) is but a dream;
>   I wish no happier one than to be laid
>   Beneath a cool syringa's scented shade,
> Or wavy willow, by the running stream,
>   Brimful of moral, where the dragon-fly
>   Wanders as careless and content as I.
> Thanks for this fancy, insect king,
> Of purple crest and filmy wing,
> Who with indifference givest up
> The water-lily's golden cup,
> To come again and overlook
> What I am writing in my book.
> Believe me, most who read the line
> Will read with hornier eyes than thine;
> And yet their souls shall live forever,
> And thine drop dead into the river!
> God pardon them, O insect king,
> Who fancy so unjust a thing!

WITH, HO! SUCH BUGS AND GOBLINS

Entered at the Post Office at New York, N. Y., at Second Class Mail Rates.

Vol. XVIII.   Published Every Week.   *Beadle & Adams, Publishers,* 98 WILLIAM STREET, N. Y., January 24, 1882.   Ten Cents a Copy. $5.00 a Year.   No. 222

BILL, THE BLIZZARD; or, Red Jack's Double Crime.

A STORY OF THE MYSTERY OF TENSPOT GULCH.

BY EDWARD WILLETT.

AUTHOR OF "BISCROFT" NOVELS," "SEAN FARLEY," ETC., ETC.

"HOLD THERE!" SHOUTED THE BLIZZARD. "FALL BACK, YOU HELLHOUNDS, OR THE PRICE OF COFFINS WILL RISE IN APACHEVILLE!"

CHAPTER VIII

A few years ago I wrote a little parable to try to make clear the quarrel of the dime novel *versus* the respectable novel. In it, a small boy was supposed to have been detected by one of the guardians of his literary morals reading one of those ancient bugbears—a dime novel. He is sent to his home in deep disgrace, accompanied by the shameful pamphlet, and also by a highly recommended and entirely proper story—to wit, "Treasure Island," which all well-informed grown-ups not only allow to children, but fairly cram down their throats. The boy's aunt and another lady, who have him in their care, open the package containing the two books and inspect them quite without either prejudice or knowledge. They are fearfully concerned because Horace has been "reading a dime novel" since they have not the least fragment of doubt that such an action is the first step which leads to the gallows in this world, and damnation in the next. Sampling the two books, in order to separate the dove from the serpent, they dip first into "Treasure Island" and naturally come upon a gory fight. Bloodshed and violence! Can there be any doubt that *this* is the well of poison? They instantly seize Stevenson's novel with the fire-tongs and carry it off to be consumed in the kitchen stove. Thus, having ridden the house of contamination, they come back to "Luck and

Pluck, or Working for the Government," the very book for which Horace was at that moment whimpering in bed, supperless. They read the opening pages of it, and find a tale so extremely chaste, ethical, and overflowing with rectitude, that they salute it as on a par with those in their own favorite magazine, the *Congregationalist Observer.*

But I wasted my pains. Nobody believed in "Luck and Pluck," although I solemnly declare that the extract which I quoted was copied verbatim from a dime— or "half-dime"—novel of that title bought by me "in the open market." Then, as now (for some horror of the dime novel still lingers, here and there, just as Beëlzebub still inspires fear), the dime novel is roundly denounced by persons who never read a page from one of them in their lives, as the cigarette is assailed by reformers like Miss Lucy Page Gaston, who very likely never smoked a whole box of cigarettes at one time in all her career.

The ancient bugaboo is always ludicrous. We can become gay over the absurd terrors suffered by our ancestors in their dread of witches, and over the ridiculous precautions they took against them. Yet it is doubtful if any of these terrors were more absurd, or any of the precautions more extravagant than those inspired in some folk of our own time by the fear of infection. When whole families have given themselves up, not as an occasional necessary measure, but as a career, as a pious exercise, to garglings, sprayings, inhalations and inoculations, in much the same ecstasy with which a Buddhist adept repeats the mystic prayer forty thousand times in succession—why should we giggle about witchcraft?

Entered at the Post Office at New York, N. Y., at Second Class Mail Rates.

Vol. XVI. Published Every Week. Beadle & Adams, Publishers, 98 WILLIAM STREET, N. Y., September 27, 1882. Ten Cents a Copy. $5.00 a Year. No. 205

THE GAMBLER PIRATE; or, Bessie, the Lady of the Lagoon,

A COMPANION STORY TO THE "SKELETON SCHOONER."

BY COL. PRENTISS INGRAHAM,

AUTHOR OF "MERLE, THE MUTINEER," "MONTEZUMA, THE MERCILESS," "FREELANCE, THE BUCCANEER," "WILD BILL, THE PISTOL DEAD SHOT," "WILD BILL'S GOLD TRAIL," ETC., ETC.

But the horror inspired by the dime novel is harder to understand. Was the firm and almost universal belief that they were "immoral" eagerly fostered and circulated, as it is asserted, by agents of some "respectable" publishing houses, to whom the immorality consisted in the fact that they sold for ten cents instead of a dollar and a half? Or was it because they were new, and popular, and therefore *must* be bad, on the theory that anything which is widely enjoyed—like the cigarette, the moving picture show, and the flapper—is necessarily wicked?

Lately I watched some of my associates in the New York Public Library prepare for exhibition more than a thousand dime novels, publications of the pioneer firm of Beadle and Adams. Books which within my own recollection had been considered an abomination, books which librarians had regarded with a shudder, to be sprinkled, metaphorically, with holy water, and thrust into the *index librorum prohibitorum*, were unblushingly, nay, proudly, placed on show, and duly ticketed as "Dime-Novels," for all to see! What strange suggestions this had of a rapid growth in intelligence.

The old style arithmetician might calculate that if all the switches, hickory sticks, straps, hair-brush backs, and other instruments of torture which have been applied by angry parents to the readers of novels in this collection should be placed "end to end" they would reach from William Street in New York, where the novels used to be published, to Cooperstown, where Erastus Beadle ended his days. And there would be enough over to lay a single track of them to Buffalo, where he first became a publisher. By the same token, if all the tears shed by distressed mothers and aunts, on discovering that their boys were "reading dime novels," should be added to the tears soon forthcoming from the boys themselves, after the traditional visit to the wood-shed with father, the resulting body of salt water would be more than enough to float not only the ship of "The Pirate Priest, or The Planter Gambler's Daughter," by Colonel Prentiss Ingraham—one of Beadle's authors—but there would also be enough for the black bark of "The Gambler Pirate, or Bessie, the Lady of the Lagoon"—another of Colonel Ingraham's novels.

By the way, let us pause a moment to admire the picture of "The Gambler Pirate," one of the later Beadle publications. It is probably by the versatile George G. White, who designed so many scores of these stirring pictures, and with liberal hand illustrated the pages of such diverse publications as the *Police Gazette* and the *Christian Herald*. The pirate chief strides the deck of his ship. His whiskers are black, curly, ambrosial. He wears a three-cornered hat, a swallow-tail coat, and tight, white breeches. But he is defied by a lady in a sort of Empire gown—with Y.W.C.A. modifications. This is the caption: "Hold, Captain Forrester! Surrender or you Die!" "God Above! You risen from the Sea, Mabel Mortimer!"

There are at least three good reasons why a public library does well to care for and to exhibit such a collection as this. The first is that the dime novel, especially as it was published by its originator, the firm of Beadle and Adams, formed an interesting by-path in the development of American literature, no less significant than the

The early type of Dime Novel

English chap-book of a century ago. It is intellectual snobbery to patronize one and to neglect the other. Second, the exhibition is an object lesson; a pathetic display of a defunct bogey. It is perpetually useful for each generation to see how much unnecessary anguish has been suffered in the past over things which were really harmless. Dime novels began as rather good historical novels; at their worst they were no more than exciting stories written sometimes, but not always, in careless English. They were never immoral; on the contrary they reeked of morality. Property rights were never confused; and when sexual ethics were involved, their standards make the modern two-dollar novel look as foul as Vulcan's stithy. Finally there are to be considered the pleasant recollections which an exhibition of this kind brought to the older generation. The old gentlemen who slipped in, looking somewhat furtively about (as if Father, with his trunk-strap, hovered near-by) and went with increasing delight from one show-case to the next, as they recalled one old friend after another—these visitors were a continual pleasure to the planners of the exhibition.

Dr. Frank O'Brien made this collection of more than thirteen hundred publications of the house of Beadle (together with some hundreds of specimens from their followers and imitators) and spent twenty years at it. Two years ago many of his duplicates were sold at auction and the prices which they brought showed that there were enthusiastic collectors, willing to pay well to fill gaps in their own sets.

Erastus F. Beadle, a descendant of American pioneers and soldiers, was born in Otsego County, New York, in

1821. Working as a boy for a miller, he found a need one day for letters of some sort to label the bags of grain. He cut the letters from blocks of hardwood, as Gutenberg's predecessors had done. This experience interested him in printing; he learned the art, and by 1852 had a printing shop of his own. In 1858 he moved to New York to test an idea which had come to him: the publication of books to be sold at ten cents, song-books, joke-books, and finally novels. He originated the dime novel, and in 1860 published the first of them, a small pamphlet with orange paper covers. The firm of Beadle and Adams continued their business until 1897, and the different forms in which their dime publications were issued are known to collectors as Type A, B, C, etc., down to Type M.

The first of these types were mainly historical novels of the American Revolution, or of early pioneer life. Among them was Edward S. Ellis's "Seth Jones," a story of frontier life in New York in 1785. More than 450,000 copies were sold. Others were Mrs. Victor's "Maum Guinea," a story of slave-life, esteemed, so it is said, by President Lincoln; "The Reefer of '76, or The Cruise of the Firefly," by Harry Cavendish; and "The Maid of Esopus, or The Trials and Triumphs of the Revolution," by N. C. Iron. With Type B, the novels assumed a cover in three colors, and a more decidedly frontier flavor: "The Prairie Scourge," "The Schuylkill Rangers," "Red Jacket, the Huron," and "Mohawk Nat" are some of the titles. About nine-tenths of the settings, then and later, were American.

By the late seventies and early eighties, the covers in

THIRD EDITION.

BEADLE'S Half Dime POCKET Library

Copyrighted, 1884, by Beadle and Adams. Entered at the Post Office at New York, N.Y., as Second Class Mail Matter. Feb. 4, 1884.

Vol. I. $2.50 a Year.   Published Weekly by Beadle and Adams, No. 98 William St., New York.   Price, Five Cents.   No. 4.

THE DOUBLE DAGGERS; Or, DEADWOOD DICK'S DEFIANCE.

BY EDWARD L. WHEELER.

DEADWOOD DICK.

black and white, and the larger magazine size, had come into use. The bison and the grizzly, cowboy and Indian, scout, trapper, road-agent and pony-express rider were the themes. These are the dime novels which many of us remember on the news-stands in our youth. I cannot sentimentalize over them, as I never read a dime novel until I was thirty, owing to a trick played upon me by my parents. They never forbade me to read dime novels at all.

Old Sleuth, Nick Carter, and Old Cap Collier were associated with other publishing firms than that of Beadle. Old Cap Collier belongs to the house of Munro. The two most famous creations of the Beadle authors were Deadwood Dick, invented by a very mild looking gentleman named Edward L. Wheeler; and Jack Harkaway, a languid dare-devil about town, of the Tom and Jerry type. Deadwood Dick, who appeared on his faithful black steed in 1884, began a series of adventures called after his name (with such titles as "Deadwood Dick on Deck, or Calamity Jane the Heroine of Whoop Up"), and was the forerunner of many alliterative heroes out of Mr. Wheeler's imagination: Omaha Oll, Photograph Phil, Corduroy Charlie, and Rosebud Rob.

Toward the end (when Type M was reached) the sensational element predominated, although such excellent authors as Captain Mayne Reid were still reprinted, and the rules of delicacy, in the treatment of elegant females —and there were never any inelegant ones—were still those of a refined seminary for young ladies. Heroines in the most distressing danger still kept the folds of their long skirts trailing upon the ground; they hunted jaguars in the South American jungles primly seated upon a side-saddle, and wearing a habit which would have been correct in Central Park in 1868. Their bathing costumes might cause their persecution for prudery today, but nothing else. But for the heroes and villains no ordinary encounter with an Indian brave, a mountain lion, or a pirate, was enough. The fight, man to man, with bowie knives, would no longer thrill the veins in 1887. No; when the outlaw hung the ranger over the cliff by his heels, the while the latter meditated whether he should give up the secret of the hidden caché, his reflections had to be stimulated by snapping crocodiles below, and hungry vultures who assailed from above. In "Double Dan the Dastard, or the Pirates of the Pécos," by Major Sam S. Hall ("Buckskin Sam"), three unfortunate persons (villains, I have no doubt) are crucified upon trees, while pumas creep toward them in the gathering gloom. We are told that "the very hair upon the captives' heads seemed to crawl like scorched serpents, and a piercing shriek, yes, shriek after shriek, sprung from the blacked and bleeding lips of each."

The dime novel had degenerated; horrors had accumulated on horror's head too many hundred times. But have the "Perils of Pauline" type of moving picture, the "Giddy Stories" type of magazine, and many of the novels of today, shown a marked improvement over them? The old devotees of the Beadle novels have an emphatic opinion on that point, and their answer is in the negative.

In order to compare the dime novel, at its most immoral, sensational and diabolical worst, with a novel

BEADLE'S Dime New York Library

COPYRIGHTED IN 1868, BY BEADLE & ADAMS.

Vol. XXII. Published Every Wednesday. *Beadle & Adams, Publishers,* 98 WILLIAM STREET, N. Y., February 6, 1884. Ten Cents a Copy. $5.00 a Year. No. 276

TEXAS CHICK, THE SOUTHWEST DETECTIVE; Or, TIGER-LILY, THE VULTURE QUEEN.

BY CAPTAIN MARK WILTON,

AUTHOR OF "CACTUS JACK," "DON SOMBRERO," "LADY JAGUAR," "THE SCORPION BROTHERS," "CANYON JOE," ETC., ETC.

"IF THEY TRY TO CLIMB HIGHER, SHOOT BOTH!" TIGER-LILY STERNLY DIRECTED.

like, say, "The Sheik," read today by thousands of highly respectable folk, I started to read "Dion the Dashing Detective, or Link after Link," by W. I. James. This was in the Old Cap Collier Library in 1883. It opens with spirit:

"By Heaven—they're lost!"

"No! No!—look there!—he's a hero—brave fellow!"

But these lines are followed by this topographical explanation:

"These exclamations were from a crowd around the northwest corner of Union Square, where Broadway, University Place, and Fourteenth Street meet. Three lines of Broadway stages round that corner. Two of the busiest lines of street cars cross each other at that point. Crowds of pedestrians converge there from all directions. . . ."

This was altogether too much like my evening walk toward home; I yearned for something more dastardly than this. Perhaps I could find it in "Night Scenes in New York; In Darkness and by Gaslight," by Old Sleuth (H. P. Halsey). This appeared in 1885. The beginning is in these words:

"In a plainly furnished room in the upper part of the City of New York, were two persons, a young girl and a fierce, bad-looking man."

Come, this is better, the upper part of the City of New York; a little farther from home. Also I like being left in no doubt about the man; he is bad-looking. Now the girl speaks:

"Back! Back! On your life, stand back!"

To which the bad-looking one makes this tame and disappointing reply:

"Adele, I love you."

She sarcastically retorts:

"And you would prove your love by acts of violence?"

But the idea is intolerable to him:

"You are wrong. I would only persuade you to be my wife."

How tame compared with "The Sheik"! The girl suggests that perhaps he is mistaken in thinking that she is "in his power." She observes that the janitor and his wife must be somewhere about. But here he shows the cloven hoof and remarks that the janitor and his wife are "creatures" of his, in his employ. Again he urges her to marry him. Listen to her defiance, her crowning effort:

"Hear me, Lyman Treadwell; I am but a poor shop-girl; my present life is a struggle for a scanty existence; my future a life of toil; but over my present life of suffering, there extends a rainbow of hope. . . . Life is short, eternity endless—the grave is but the entrance to eternity. And you, villain! ask me to change my present peace for a life of horror with you. No, monster, rather may I die at once!"

At this point a comic German, with a revolver, breaks in and rescues the girl. But I had no further interest in either of them. No matter how "bad-looking" he might be, a monster named Lyman Treadwell could not excite my sympathy nor aversion. Anybody who would stand still under an oration like that is too stodgy to satisfy my requirements for a villain.

THIRD EDITION.

ENTERED AT THE POST OFFICE AT NEW YORK, N. Y., AT SECOND CLASS MAIL RATES.

Vol. XX. Published Every Week. Beadle & Adams, Publishers, 98 WILLIAM STREET, N. Y., September 19, 1883. Ten Cents a Copy. $5.00 a Year. No. 256

DOUBLE DAN, THE DASTARD; or, THE PIRATES OF THE PECOS.

BY MAJOR SAM S. HALL—"Buckskin Sam."

AUTHOR OF "DIAMOND DICK," "THE LONE STAR GAMBLER," "THE TERRIBLE TONKAWAY," "KIT CARSON, JR.," "BIG FOOT WALLACE," ETC.

THE VERY HAIR UPON THE CAPTIVES' HEADS SEEMED TO CRAWL LIKE SCORCHED SERPENTS, AND A PIERCING SHRIEK—THE SHRIEK AFTER AGONY—SPRUNG FROM THE CRACKED AND BLEEDING LIPS OF EACH.

THE CARY GIRLS

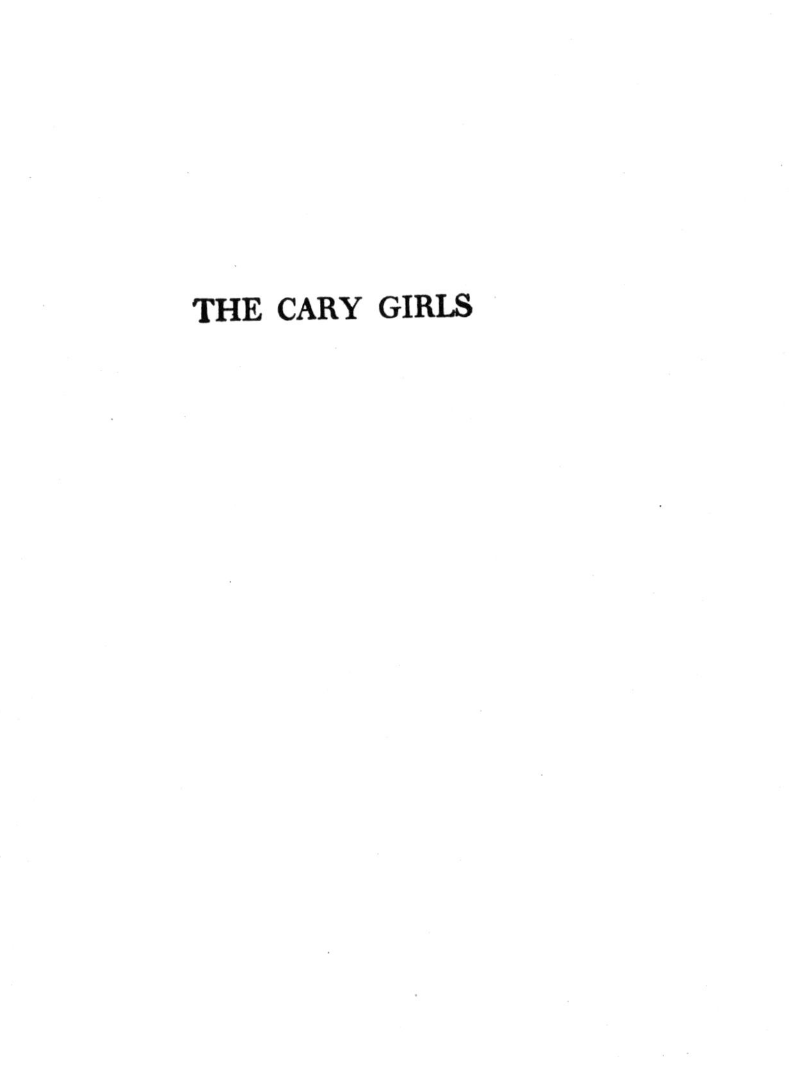

CHAPTER IX

There was once a bashful old professor of literature at Yale, who ended a course of lectures on American writers by uttering a deprecatory cough, and an apology. "Gentlemen," he explained, "when I commenced these lectures, I intended if time allowed, to embrace both Phoebe and Alice Cary."

As I write this, I am sitting at a window from which I have many times seen the Cary sisters—their blue veils flying—go by to their work. Not Phoebe and Alice, but Miss Hattie and Miss Ellen Cary, who were much concerned with the art of literature in our town.

The Twentieth Century has altered Lanesport. The town hall where we used to see Ullie Akerstrom, "Lanesport's Favorite Actress," in "Uncle Tom's Cabin" (with the blood-hounds led through the street in procession before the show), is now a Community Hall, housing the Plaza Picture Palace. Mrs. Bagley's millinery establishment is replaced by the Up-To-Date Garage; and Mr. Davenport's little shop, with its low and dingy ceiling, where he would sell you delicious molasses candy, or open at your demand innumerable oysters which he or his son had taken from their beds early that morning— this place now appears with flamboyant decoration and enlarged area as Kondokoupolos Brothers' House of Sweets. But more than anything I resent the transformation of Miss Cary's circulating library into La Fortune's Phonograph Parlor and Souvenir Post-card Emporium.

About twenty minutes before nine every morning the Cary girls would trot down our street, Miss Hattie to open the reading-room in the public library, and Miss Ellen to her own little circulating library, where she sat all morning and afternoon, renting books at two cents a day. They were white-haired women when I first knew them, but they had never married, and so by the custom of the town, they were and would remain the "Cary *girls*," even though they lived to four-score and ten.

Miss Hattie was tall and slender; Miss Ellen, short and stout. Miss Ellen might have posed for Queen Victoria. Indeed, some years later, when the fashion for "Living Pictures" reached Lanesport, I am not sure she was not induced to put on a black gown and a widow's cap, and impersonate that diminutive and dignified monarch. Both sisters parted their hair in the middle, and wore long blue cloaks in summer and "fur-lined circulars" in the winter. Their bonnets were not unlike those now worn by the Salvation Army girls, except that they were complicated by the windings of yards and yards of blue veils.

You may be inclined to dismiss them as a couple of "New England old maids," since spinsters, it is well known, exist only in New England. They appear to you, perhaps, as relics of that Puritanism which so many people are now engaged in deriding. But it is not in this light that I remember them. They had their standards and their limitations, and their points of conservatism, but that they were just as eager for human progress as many of the platitudinous "liberals" and "radicals" who haunt the book-shops of Greenwich Village, there is not in my mind an atom of doubt.

Like those radicals, they were opposed to bloodshea. But instead of the healthy and necessary bloodshed of Germans in Belgium and France—which so disturbed the radicals—the trial of brute force which horrified Miss Hattie and Miss Ellen was the projected fight between John L. Sullivan and Corbett in New Orleans. They thought it disgraceful that such a spectacle should be allowed "in this nineteenth century." They grieved at my interest in it. But when I met them, on my way to school the morning after the fight, their concerted, excited, and altogether human inquiry was: "Who won the fight?"

Miss Ellen Cary's circulating library was all contained in a small room. The walls were lined and the floor-space covered with book-cases and the books were protected and disguised by brown-paper covers. Surely *The Purple Pagan*, the radical book-shop near Washington Square, which I occasionally visit nowadays, is a brighter, more vivid, and apparently more exciting place. But for all its color and uneasy exploitation of various egotisms, it does not inspire my imagination as much as Miss Cary's dismal-looking collection. And this is curious, since all its art is supposed to set the imagination afire; its sculptors scorn to model more of a human figure than an elbow sticking out of a solid block of clay. Your imagination is called upon to supply the rest of the figure.

In Miss Cary's library you stood and wondered what was behind those paper covers. What strange voyage or extraordinary chapters of wonder might be disclosed if you took one of those volumes home? There had been some great moments. A tale of a suicide club, and the story of a rajah's diamond had been found in one called "The New Arabian Nights," by a Scotchman whose life was then drawing to a close in the South Sea Islands. There were some crisp and tingling little stories about India by a newspaper man from Lahore, who had just offended America by his flippant account of his visit to this country. My brother had recently come home with two poems which he had committed to memory—two extraordinary poems which filled me with delight. They were also by this newspaper man from India, and they were called "Gunga Din" and "Mandalay." And for the next ten years I never hesitated to horrify my elders by saying that Kipling and Stevenson were far better than Sir Walter Scott. Now it is my turn to be horrified and disgusted when I hear that boys in school and college think that only old fogies read Kipling and Stevenson. Who is better? I tremulously cry. Not ——? or ——? Don't make me laugh!

Miss Cary lent me a book called "The Three Impostors," by Arthur Machen (who had been reading "The New Arabian Nights," I could see), and it was very much to my taste. The proprietor of *The Purple Pagan* has just discovered Arthur Machen (more than twenty-five years after Miss Ellen Cary) and offers me his books at a fancy price.

It would be wrong to say that the Cary girls have no representatives today. There is Mr. Falcon, the owner of a quiet book-shop in New York. He is the gravest book-dealer in the city. He raises his head from his desk and surveys me with his mild blue eyes. He bows courteously as I come in his shop, and asks how he may serve me. His hair and beard are so fine and silvery that I would liken him to an etching by—but I never can remember who did the etching. The Curator of Prints, to whom I submitted the question, says that Seymour Haden is not the man. The Curator does not know my old book-dealer, and I am shaky about Seymour Haden. So the point may never be settled.

"I would like to look about," I tell the book-dealer.

"Is there some subject in which you are particularly interested?"

There are fifteen subjects, and this news is imparted to the dealer. He shows polite disbelief and fatherly amusement. I am still under sixty, and I can see that the old book-dealer thinks it distressing that so young a reader should play with the truth. I mention one or two of my interests, but it does no good. He regards them as frivolous. Mine is not a case needing learned guidance. Jimmie—who is about thirteen—is called, and instructed to lead me to see some of the books I have indicated. Jimmie and I walk down the shop together, and I feel grateful not to be given a fairy-tale and told to trot away home.

It is not surprising that many book-dealers arrive at this frame of mind. Shyness in the presence of books is not peculiar to one side of the counter.

The older and more experienced dealers may carry too far their manner of paternal tolerance for the limitations of the young. I knew a girl who was attracted by the pretty edition of "The Compleat Angler," edited by Mr. Le Gallienne, and published a dozen years ago by Mr. Lane. Happening to be in a strange city—famed for its book-shops—she decided to buy a copy as a gift. She was neither wrinkled, gray, nor be-spectacled—far from any of these—but she had spent two or three years in the order division of a public library, during its organization, and more books new and old had passed through her hands and under her observation in a week than the clerks in the book-shop to which she applied were apt to handle in a month. A nice old gentleman came to wait on her, and to him she mentioned her wish, saying that it was a new edition, and adding some details about it.

His eyes twinkled behind his gold eye-glasses. Here was a funny story to tell his friends. This pretty young school girl, who had gone about as far into literature as Richard Harding Davis's romances! His voice was so soothing as he replied, that she expected him to pat her hands.

"My dear young lady," said he, prolonging the word "dear," " 'The Compleat Angler' is a very, *very* old book, written a great many years ago——"

"Yes, I know," she interrupted, "but there is a new edition——"

"By Izaak Walton," he continued, and having informed her so far, and wagging his head in a sort of solemn merriment, to show that he was not angry at her preposterous inquiry, he fairly backed her out of the shop, closed the door, and left her to go and acquire age and wisdom.

My searches in the shop of the old dealer are not often successful. As soon as Jimmie and I pass the section near the door, devoted to novels of the present year, we are immersed in the Black Walnut period of American literature. That fascinating decade when Andrew Lang and Austin Dobson were writing ballades, when Frank Stockton was writing and A. B. Frost picturing the comedies of American country life—this pleasant era seems to be despised by my old gentleman. He has no past except that of the Beecher trial and the Danbury News Man. I may buy a biography of Adoniram Judson, if I wish, or "Dred, a Tale of the Great Dismal Swamp." Miss Madeleine Smith, the Glasgow beauty, read the latter, by the way, about the year after its publication, and nearly at the same time when she was refreshing her lover, M. L'Angelier, with cocoa thoughtfully mixed (so it was asserted) with arsenic. She did not enjoy the novel, but it was all the amusement she had on a rainy Sunday.

It is a matter of fifty-one blocks in distance to *The Purple Pagan*, and the change is from Clarissa Harlowe to Ann Veronica. The place is bright with new book-covers, and posters full of yellows and greens. It is the "greenery-yallery, Grosvenor Gallery" school of English æstheticism, dished up again forty years later and enlivened by one jigger of Cubism, one of Vorticism, a dash of Communism, the whole mingled with that which Keats long ago saw upon a Grecian urn two thousand years old —the spirit of youth, "forever panting and forever young."

It is all giddy and bright and a little loony. Here comes Alys, the very spirit of America's Bohemia. Born in Nebraska, she has moved to New York "to live her own life." To her fellow-townsmen this suggests awful memories of George Sand and her carryings on, but it really means nothing worse than dining when she feels so inclined on chocolate caramels, cooked on an alcohol flame in the bath-tub. She has a dear friend called Bernice who is even more modern. Back in 1920 I saw Bernice one afternoon turning into Eighth Street; she was dressed in a kind of green burlap. She wore no stockings but had carefully painted pansies on her ankles. Two dogs backed growling into an area as she passed by, and a baby in a perambulator, seeing her, set up a terrific howl. "I hope you don't think we dress with *attractiveness* in mind!" she said to her brother, who had come on to visit her. "Well, what do you dress for?" he replied faintly; "political reasons?"

Poor Bernice! She is so busy in being modern that there is no chance that she will ever discover how ancient she really is. As she is vowed never to read anything a year old she will never see herself as Lady Jane, Angela, Saphir and all the others in W. S. Gilbert's "Patience." Yet there she was forty years ago, green burlap and all,— or as Lady Jane said: "a cobwebby grey velvet, with a tender bloom like cold gravy, which made Florentine Fourteenth Century, trimmed with Venetian leather and

Spanish altar lace, and surmounted with something Japanese—it matters not what—" And Bernice has much in common with Mrs. Cimabue Brown, a creation of a social satirist named Du Maurier, of whom, however, she has never heard. *She* offended the eye with peacock-feathers; Bernice does it with *batik;* but they look alike as two string-beans.

Alys and Bernice are much "intrigued" (for they still use that base-born verb) by Morris, who came a few years ago, when he was fifteen, from southern Russia. There he had to be revolutionary in order not to be classed with the stupid and illiterate. Here he keeps on being revolutionary to prove that he is still intellectual, and as nobody asks him what he wishes to revolutionize, the mental effort is almost negligible. Looking about for tyrants, he descries in the President another Nicholas II, and thinks that the Governor of New York is practically as good, for his purposes, as the old Procurator of the Holy Synod. All the people he knew in southern Russia were very gloomy, and he is convinced that it is so with the Americans. An annoying cheerfulness, which is sometimes forced upon his attention, is easily dismissed. The Intellectuals are not that way, he reflects. For reasons connected with his digestion, it is not difficult for Morris to fight off cheerfulness, and so there he is, both intellectual and pessimistic, without the slightest exertion.

And yet they are uneasy. Alys and Morris and Bernice are perpetually uncomfortable, are suffering pangs which are no part of their programme. Partly this is because they need exercise and a change from eccentric food. The biliousness of their art is symbolic. But their troubles are deeper than that; they live in constant dread, —dread of being conventional, of being called Puritanical or Mid-Victorian. Life is difficult in a circle where the rules for poetry or painting are laid down anew each Monday afternoon, upset by another authority on Wednesday in favor of a new code of laws, which are, in turn, declared Mid-Victorian on Thursday morning. Like a girl from the country, who dreads to be called a prude, and so hastens to light a cigarette before she has even had time to get settled at her table in a Bohemian restaurant, they have subjected themselves to a tyranny of ideas as cruel as those of the Puritans.

The books which cover the tables in *The Purple Pagan,* fresh, bright, and attractive—show that the writers are fearful that somebody may not remember that "male and female created He them." There has been a lapse into forgetfulness about sex on the part of the human race, it appears, and something ought to be published on the subject. Here are a few attempts to supply the want. But they scream a little too loud. They forever want to tell somebody "the facts of life." Like the old lady who wakened her confessor at two in the morning, to confess her one sin, which was committed fifty years ago, they "likes to talk about it." Their liberalism is a tight little doctrine which keeps its hottest hatred for liberals of other stripes. Toward the arch-Tories of the world they are more than friendly. Their pacifism objects to the shedding of blood in any formal manner. But a bomb tossed nonchalantly into a crowd, or the shooting of unarmed men in the back—since these re-quire no degrading drill nor discipline on the part of the performer—are perfectly tolerable to them. To keep their own skins whole and safe is their notion of the noblest conduct,—and they call themselves "idealists" forty times a day. Their novelists hold up the slacker, the sneak, and the deserter for sympathy and admiration; their story-tellers discuss their own bodily functions as if they were old grannies gossiping in a sanatorium, or wheezy clubmen with disordered livers. And this senile chatter is hailed, in *The Purple Pagan*, as "the cry of youth."

On the whole, the worst thing about them is their complexions. They are as sallow as their paintings, as puffy and muddy as their clay and wax figurines. Old Mr. Falcon, with his bright blue eyes and pink cheeks, looks as if he could give Morris ten yards in a hundred yard dash. Morris, I believe, claimed exemption in 1918, not because he objected to putting bullets into other men, nor was afraid some other man might put a bullet into him. But the thought of being made to get up early and take some exercise revolted his proud soul. His personal freedom to remain a little greasy looking was in danger. An hour's drill and a shower-bath would brighten his views on politics, art, and literature. But he would denounce me as a militarist and a slave to capitalism if I told him so. And he would smile a sad, greenish smile to show what he thinks of the mental equipment of cheerful persons.

As for the comparative liberality of their literary notions—I suppose it must be admitted that *The Purple Pagan* is much narrower than Miss Cary. They both have their crotchets. Miss Cary disapproved of "Peck's Bad Boy" for persons of my age, and so inspired me with an unholy desire to read it. She did or she did not— I really cannot remember—keep solely for her older readers a little book by Grant Allen, called "The Woman Who Did," which (laughable to recall) was then sold, after whispered conversations and with a great show of secrecy, by newsboys on the trains. Today it sits neglected on the book-shelves, middle-aged, obscure, and only occasionally sought for its Aubrey Beardsley title-page.

The Purple Pagan is still devoted to the theory that to be in trouble with the police is the sign of the artist. The proprietor of that gaudy shop always patronizes Poe, not on account of his poetry, for that is diametrically opposed to all the Pagan's ideas of verse-making, but because of his enjoyment of the belief that Poe was a drunkard. Nothing could be more amusing than to have Poe come back, sit at his editorial desk for a week, and release the torrent of his critical rage upon the *vers librists* and others of their stripe.

Miss Cary first brought to my notice the fact that the current *Lippincott's Magazine* had in it a yarn of a new and admirable detective who dosed himself with cocaine and owned a friend named Watson. At about that time there appeared in the same magazine a weird story, slightly sweet, slightly sickish, called "The Picture of Dorian Gray." Miss Cary said that the author was a donkey, but that he could write. She lent me a novel called "Tess of the d'Urbervilles," but at that time it seemed to me to have "too much scenery" in it. Aside from a murder and a hanging there was little to attract me. Miss Cary had not yet heard—and neither had any one of us—of an Irish critic named Shaw; perhaps a curious, thin book named "The Time Machine," by H. G. Wells, had come to her library. If so, knowing my tastes, she certainly passed it on to me. Mark Twain had just published a book—with delightful illustrations —which I enjoyed then as I have never been able to enjoy it since. It was "The Connecticut Yankee." Miss Cary talked less about liberalism but believed in it rather more than the Purple man does. She allowed authors freedom in choice of subject; he would pin them down to a pretty narrow range. The themes of both "Othello" and "Macbeth" were great themes in her opinion; *The Purple Pagan* would vote for "Othello" and despise the theme of "Macbeth." She cared not at all about the politics of a novelist or a poet, but he would insist that even the writer of nursery rhymes must believe in Communism, or whatever cure-all he happened to favor at the moment. If Miss Cary were Czar, I think it would be an easy sort of tyranny, but one has only to look at the fanatic's eyes of *The Purple Pagan* to know that his firing-squads would never stop until they had cleared the earth of all who did not share his beliefs, down to his last economic or artistic dogma.

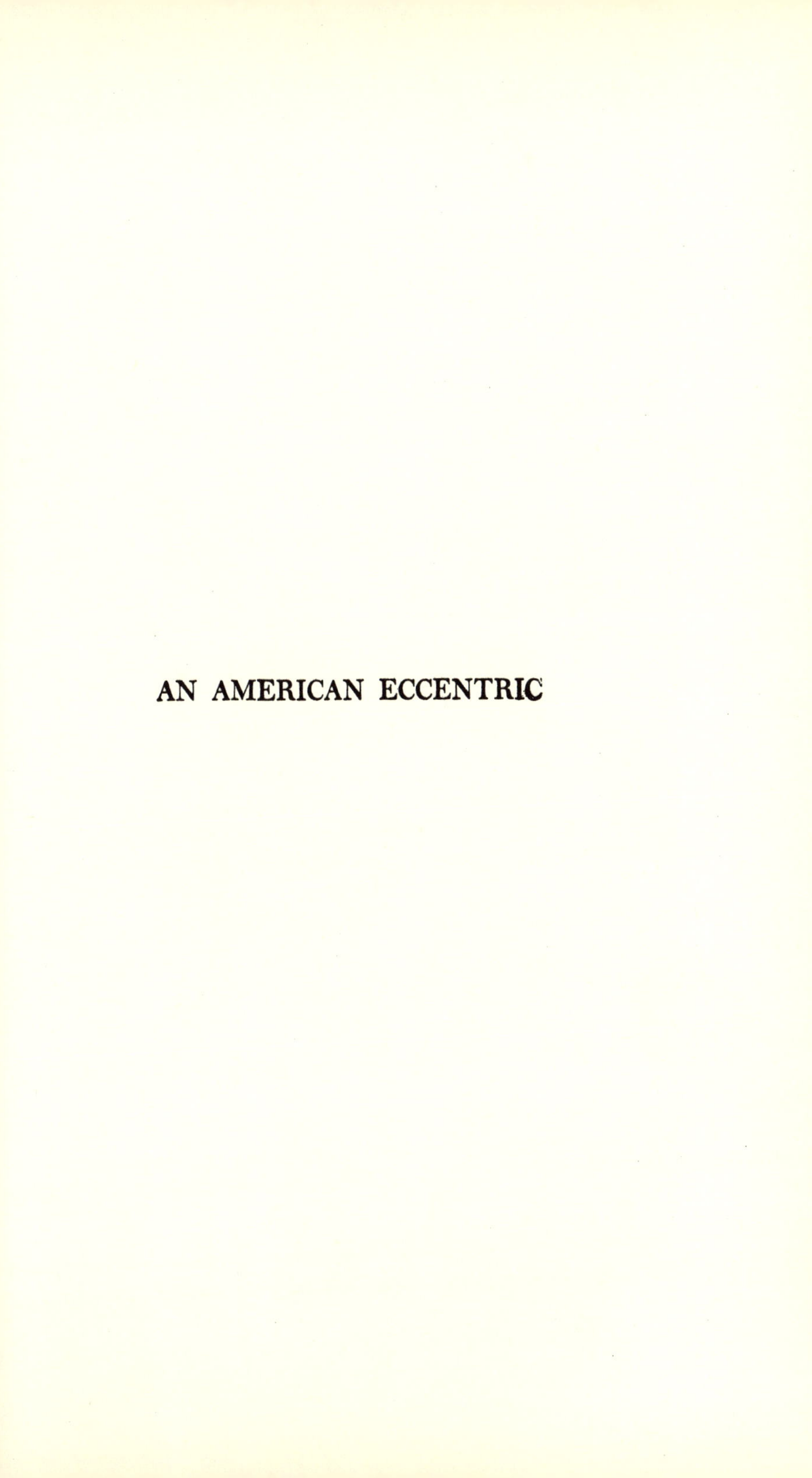

AN AMERICAN ECCENTRIC

CHAPTER X

Many of the "English Eccentrics" in John Timbs' book of that name, were residents of London, or were directly connected with that city. The absence of any city in America, at once the capital and the metropolis, may have done something to prevent that kind of notoriety which is essential to the discovery of a genuine "eccentric." The person who is actually distinguished for any reason, but who happens to possess certain curious traits or habits, the man about whom a few anecdotes are related, is not correctly called an eccentric. Indeed, genuine fame, resting upon achievement, takes its owner out of this odd class. Nor is the peculiar man or woman, of purely local celebrity, who has always existed in every city, town, and village, an eccentric within the meaning of the term. His oddities must be his chief claim to attention, and he must be known, more or less, throughout the nation.

It is hard indeed, to name a parallel to a strange personage who flourished in Massachusetts in the first years of the republic. He was an early, and, to his neighbors, rather objectionable example of the newly rich, and of the innumerable legends which clustered about his name, four or five became celebrated all over the country. At least two of these were indisputable, while some of the others are apparently founded upon reliable tradition.

Some of them still linger in the memory of local historians, and one at least, was once widely known among bibliographers, printers, and collectors of curious Americana. Timothy Dexter's assumption of the title of "Lord," his house with its wooden statues, his alleged success in strange speculations—especially in the shipment of warming-pans to the West Indies—and finally his pamphlet, "A Pickle for the Knowing Ones," with its famous addendum in the later editions, gave him the stature of a full-sized eccentric, no less interesting than any of those in John Timbs' work.

Timothy Dexter—the name is admirably suited—was born in Malden, Massachusetts, January 22, 1747-48, and came to Newburyport in 1769. In this town Dexter lived nearly all the rest of his life; he died in 1806. It was one of the important sea-ports of the United States. Samuel Eliot Morison writes, in "The Maritime History of Massachusetts":

> Newburyport specialized in the Labrador and Bay fisheries, in which sixty vessels were engaged in 1806. Her other hundred and sixteen vessels were employed in coasting, West Indian and European trade—of which more anon. Newburyport was also noted for rum and whiskey distilleries, for Laird's ale and porter, and for goldsmiths; Jacob Perkins having discovered a cheap method of making gold-plated beads, which were then in fashion. Even after the war-time depression there were ten jewelers' and watchmakers' shops at Newburyport. Here were printed and published the numerous editions of Bowditch's "Navigator," and Captain Furlong's "American Coast Pilot." *

* The "great fire" of 1811 destroyed 250 buildings, including four printing offices, four book-shops (in one of which the loss was $30,000) and the town library.—E. L. P.

Newburyport boasted a society inferior to that of no other town on the continent. Most of the leading families were but one generation removed from the plough or the forecastle; but they had acquired wealth before the Revolution, and conducted social matters with the grace and dignity of an old régime. When Governor Gore, in 1809, made a state visit to Newburyport, where he had once studied law, he came in coach and four with outriders, uniformed aides, and a cavalry escort; and when the town fathers informed his ancient benefactress, Madame Atkins, that His Excellency would honor her with a call, the spokesman delivered his message on his knees at the good lady's feet. We read of weekly balls and routs, of wedding coaches drawn by six white horses with liveried footmen, in this town of less than eight thousand inhabitants. When personal property was assessed, several Newburyport merchants reported from one thousand to twelve hundred gallons of wine in their cellars.

Federalist architecture has here left perhaps her finest permanent trace. High Street, winding along a ridge commanding the Merrimack, rivals Chestnut Street of Salem, despite hideous interpolations of the late Nineteenth Century. The gambrel-roofed type lasted into the seventeen-nineties, when the Newburyport merchants began to build square, three-storied, hip-roofed houses of brick, surrounded with ample grounds, gardens and "housins." The ship carpenters who (if tradition is correct) designed and built these houses, adopted neither the graceful porches nor the applied Adam detail of McIntire; but their tooled mouldings on panel, cornice, and chimneypiece have a graceful and original vigor.

Dexter seems alternately to have amused and annoyed the people of the town in which he rose to notoriety. His business was that of leather-dresser, and dealer in hides; his social position was humble. As early as 1776, and possibly as a joke, he was elected "Informer" by the legal voters. The duties of this office concerned the enforcement of the law in regard to killing deer,—probably it was not a post that entailed much labor. Curiously enough, the game laws of Massachusetts were so successful in protecting deer that a century after the death of Timothy Dexter the appearance of wild deer within the city limits of Newburyport was not infrequent, and the State Legislature made an annual appropriation for the benefit of farmers in various parts of the State, whose crops and trees were injured by these protected animals.

At the end of the Revolutionary War, Dexter made a profitable investment in the depreciated currency, which was afterward redeemed at par by the government. This was probably the foundation of his fortune. For about five years, beginning in 1791, he owned and lived in what was known as the Tracy mansion. It is now occupied by the public library. He began to take himself seriously as a "merchant prince," as a local oracle, and as a host. His habits with wine and spirits were expansive, even for that period, although he always made it a point to be sober in the morning, for the transaction of business. His lack of settled or orthodox religious views offended a church-going community, and it is probable that his followers and associates were gay young men, and semi-reputable citizens who were willing to flatter him, to drink his wines, eat his dinners, and laugh at his peculiarities. He made a number of offers of public benefactions; he gave money to one of the churches and a bell, which bears his name, to another of them.

The story runs that one of the deacons of this church gave a number of silver dollars to be cast with the bell, and insure its silvery tone. I am afraid something happened to those dollars; too many times I have had my melancholy increased on hot Sunday afternoons and evenings by the jangling of this bell to think of it as silvery. Curiously enough, though, it seemed to me to make a joyful noise when I used to be allowed to help ring it on February 22nd and July 4th.

Dexter offered to pave the principal street, if it should be renamed in his honor, and to build for the town a market-house. The town disliked to accept him as a benefactor, and declined with thanks. Miffed at this slight, he moved to Chester, New Hampshire, where he lived for two years.

In 1798, however, he returned to Newburyport and bought the large, three-story house on High Street, which was to be known as the Dexter House from that time to the present. Oliver Wendell Holmes mentions it in "Elsie Venner." His decorations made it grotesque, but now they are removed, the house remains as one of the best types of the Georgian or so-called "Colonial" domestic architecture, rivalling Lowell's home at Elmwood, and the Craigie-Longfellow house in Cambridge.

Dexter's family life was unhappy, and in a few months he was advertising the house for sale in the following words:

To be Sold

That elegant Mansion House situate in Newbury Port, owned by the subscriber, together with about Nine Acres of Land adjoining, with the Out Houses, Stores, Stables, etc. The House has a new Cupola, with a spread eagle on the top, which turns with the wind; finished in an elegant manner, and perhaps makes as good an appearance as any Seat in the United States. There are in the garden about 150

Fruit Trees, which produce a great plenty of fruit, and good Well of Water.

In one of the banks of the Garden is an elegent new Tomb, on the top of which is erected the Temple of Reason, 12 feet square, 11 feet high, with 158 squares of glass in it. Likewise.

All my Household Furniture and Plate, which is equal to the House. Also my Coach Horses and Carriages; payment made easy; one-third down the other in three years, with interest and good security. Any gentleman wishing to purchase the above may hear of the terms by applying to the subscriber, living on the premises.

TIMOTHY DEXTER.*

Who built the "elegent new Tomb"? It sounds like Dexter; he afterwards wished to be buried in it. But he must have worked rapidly; he bought the house August 15, 1798, and here he is advertising it for sale on the following January 2nd, tomb and all, complete. The previous owner had been a highly respectable sea-captain and privateer, Thomas Thomas; he seems an unlikely person to build a tomb with a "Temple of Reason" on top, especially since he was a vestryman of St. Paul's Church! The house had been built more than twenty years earlier by Jonathan Jackson, also a worthy citizen, a member of the Continental Congress.

But Dexter never made the sale; he lived in the house until his death, seven years later. His thoughts turning upon the end of this mortal life, he celebrated a mock-funeral for himself. Some hundreds of curious persons attended,—Dexter wrote: "it was a solemn day, there was much Cring [crying] about three thousand spectators." The tradition is that Dexter watched the funeral

* *Columbian Centinel* (Boston), January 2, 1799.

from an upper window, and afterwards beat his wife because she did not shed enough tears.

In 1801 he contracted (driving a hard bargain), with Joseph Wilson, a young ship-carver, for the wooden statues, painted in bright colors, which he placed on pillars and arches in front of his house. In the local newspaper Dexter gave a preliminary list of these statues:

> The 3 presidents, Doctor franklin, John hen Cock, and Mr Hamilton and Rouffous King and John Jea, and 2 grane-dears on the top of the hous, 4 Lions below, 1 Eagel, is on the Coupulow, one Lamb to lay down with one of the Lions,—One Yonnecorne, one Dogg, Addam and Eave in the garden,—one horse. The houll [whole] is not concluded on as yet.

In 1802 appeared his pamphlet "A Pickle for the Knowing Ones." He had already been called "Lord" Timothy Dexter, and had included himself in the statues in front of his house, with the inscription "I am the first in the East, the first in the West, and the greatest philosopher in the known world." Jonathan Plummer was appointed his poet laureate, and rewarded with a small salary, a suit of livery, a large cocked-hat, and gold-headed cane. These are the opening stanzas of one of the laureate's odes, certainly better verses than one usually expects from an eccentric poet in a small town:

> To Sir Timothy Dexter, on his returning to Newbury-port, after residing a long time at Chester in New Hampshire, a congratulatory Ode: by Jonathan Plummer, Junr., Poet Lauriet to his Lordship.

Your Lordship's welcome back again—
  Fair nymphs with sighs have mourn'd your staying
So long from them and me your swain,
  And wonder'd at such long delaying;
But now you bless again our eyes,
Our melting sorrow droops and dies.

The town of Chester to a Lord
  Must seem a desert dull and foggy,
A gloomy place—upon my word
  I think it dirty, wet and boggy:
Far different from your Kingly seat,*
In good saint James his famous street.

In 1805 James Akin engraved and published a portrait of Dexter, reproduced with this chapter. The dog, which seems to have amazed all who have commented upon Dexter, combining as he did the engaging qualities of the pig, the dachshund, and the bat, is always described as "hairless" and "peculiar." Probably he was a Mexican hairless dog.

The notice of Timothy Dexter's death, from the *Newburyport Herald*, was as follows:

Departed this life, on Wednesday evening last (October 22, 1806) Mr. Timothy Dexter, in the 60th year of his age,—self-styled "Lord Dexter, first in the East." He lived perhaps one of the most eccentric men of his time. His singularities and peculiar notions were universally proverbial. Born and bred in a low condition in life, and his intellectual endowments not being of the most exalted stamp, it is no wonder that a splendid fortune, which he acquired (though perhaps honestly) by dint of speculation and good fortune, should have rendered him, in many respects, truly

* Kingly seat—The elegant house in saint James his park and street, which belonged sometime since to Jonathan Jackson, Esq.—Plummer's note.

TIMOTHY DEXTER AND HIS DOG.

ridiculous. The qualities of his mind were of that indefinite cast which forms an exception to every other character recorded in history, or known in the present age, and "none but himself could be his parallel." But among the motley groups of his qualities, it would be injustice to say he possessed no good ones—he certainly did. No one will impeach his honesty, and his numerous acts of liberality, both public and private, are in the recollection of all, while one of the items in his last Will will be gratefully remembered. His ruling passion appeared to be popularity, and one would suppose he rather chose to render his name "infamously famous than not famous at all." His writings stand as a monument of the truth of this remark; for those who have read his "Pickle for the Knowing Ones," a jumble of letters promiscuously gathered together, find it difficult to determine whether most to laugh at the consummate folly, or despise the vulgarity and profanity of the writer. His manner of life was equally extravagant and singular. A few years since he erected in front of his house a great number of images of distinguished persons in Europe and America, together with beasts, etc., so that his seat exhibited more the appearance of a museum of artificial curiosities than the dwelling of a family. By his orders a tomb was several years since dug under the summer house in his garden, where he desired his remains might be deposited (but this singular request could not consistently be complied with), and his coffin made and kept in the hall of his house, in which he is to be buried. The fortunate and singular manner of his speculations, by which he became possessed of a handsome property, are well known, and his selling a cargo of warming-pans to the W. Indies, where they were converted into molasses-ladles and sold to a good profit, is but one of the most peculiar. His principles of religion (if they could be called principles) were equally odd: a blind philosophy peculiar to himself led him to believe in the system of transmigration at some times; at others he expressed those closely connected with deism; but it is not a matter of surprise that one so totally illiterate should have no settled or rational principles. His reason left him two days before his death, but he has gone to render an account of his life to a just and merciful judge.

The funeral of Mr. Dexter will be to-morrow, at 3 o'clock, from his dwelling house.

This not too flattering tribute (in which, by the way, Dexter is named as the tomb builder) sounds as if it were written by some local clergyman. Dexter had quarreled with one of them and perhaps given cause for offence. He also criticized, justly enough, their tendency to quarrel with one another. The doubt expressed in this obituary notice of the final destination of Dexter's soul was not repeated in the funeral oration by his poet laureate. Poor, eccentric Jonathan Plummer published in the same year, a broadside, called "Something New." It was a miscellany of information about Dexter, ending with a sermon in which he expressed a belief that his patron's charity (one of Dexter's benevolences was a bequest of $2000 for the poor of the town, the first bequest of the kind in Newburyport) would help blot out his faults, and that he would ultimately rest in "the glorious company of Abraham, Isaac and Jacob." The imagination balks at the picture of Timothy Dexter making one of this *partie carrée*, but Plummer's theology is perhaps as good as that of the pedant who prepared the notice for the *Newburyport Herald*.

The total value of Dexter's estate was about $35,000, no mean sum in 1806, even in a town whose size and importance in the United States at that time was equal to that of Baltimore or San Francisco today. His last will and testament was wise and philanthropic—so that it could be truthfully said on his grave-stone in the bury-

By permission David McKay Co.

The Dexter House about 1805

(From an illustration by James Preston in Paul M. Hollister's "Famous Colonial Houses")

ing-ground (after the board of health refused to allow his burial on his own estate) :

> He gave liberal Donations
> For the support of the Gospel:
> For the benefit of the Poor,
> And for other benevolent purposes.

In regard to the speculation in warming-pans, Dexter, in the second edition of his "Pickle" (1805) begins one paragraph with the words, "How Did Dexter make his money. . . ." He names three speculations, one in whalebone, one in Bibles (called alternately "the bibbel" and the "bibel") and one in warming-pans. Of the last he writes merely this:

> . . . one more ſpect Drole A Nouf I Dreamed of worming pans three Nits that they would doue in the weſt inges I got not more than fortey two thouſand put them in Nine veſſels for difrent ports that tuck good hold—I cleared sevinty nine per sent—the pans thay mad yous of them for Coucking . . .

The usual story is that the warming-pans were employed for ladling molasses—their natural use being superfluous in the "west inges." But the historical student has laid his chilling hand upon these warming-pans. William C. Todd, in a paper called "Timothy Dexter" (1886), expressed doubts of all these speculations, as well as of another apocryphal tale of a shipment of a cargo of *mittens* to the West Indies, which were diverted to Russia, and sold there at great profit. Of the most celebrated venture, Mr. Todd writes:

His next most noted speculation was in sending 42,000 warming-pans to the West Indies. No hard-ware was made in this country until a little more than half a century ago, and all the warming-pans in use came from Great Britain. The amount named would have cost about $150,000, to be paid for in hard money, as bills of exchange were then but little used. Such an importation and exportation would have required months of time, and would have made a sensation indeed, for, though common, a large part of the families had none, and they are now rare as old curiosities. Is it possible, rating his intelligence very low, that, if he had attempted such a speculation, he would not have been persuaded of its folly long before he could have executed it? Except for the purpose for which they were made, they are of no value. Dexter says they were sold in the West Indies as cooking utensils, but a glance shows how inconvenient they would be for such use. The tradition is that they were sold to dip and strain molasses, but they are poorly adapted to this, and nearly a century ago, when sugar plantations were few in the West Indies, but a small part of 42,000 would have satisfied any such demand. Did any visitor to the West Indies ever see or hear of one of these 42,000 warming-pans?

Of the editions and reprints of Dexter's "A Pickle for the Knowing Ones" I have seen nine; it is not unlikely that there were others. The first edition (1802) is a small pamphlet, about four by six inches, with 24 pages. Its title-page and two other pages are reproduced here. The author describes the statues which he was placing in front of his house, and his own tribulations—such as receiving "hard Noks on my head 4 difrent times from a Boy to this Day." He makes his announcement: "Ime the first Lord in the younited States of Amercary Now of Newburyport it is the voise of the peopel and I cant Help it. . . ." He discusses religion and local affairs, and

A

PICKLE

FOR THE

KNOWING ONES:

OR

PLAIN TRUTHS

IN A

HOMESPUN DRESS.

By TIMOTHY DEXTER, Esq.

SALEM:

PRINTED FOR THE AUTHOR.
1802.

First Edition

ends, "The follering peases are not my Riting but very drole,"—which serves as an introduction to a brief anecdote about Indians, and to a sermon by an English clergyman on the subject of robbery, a topic upon which Dexter, as a man of property and owner of an orchard, was especially sensitive. Dexter's language, in a few passages of this edition, is gross, and these passages are repeated in the second edition (1805) published in his life-time. In one of the later editions (1838) the editor has protected his readers from contamination by the device of asterisks.

In 1805 there were printed two more editions, differing from each other, and both of them larger than the first edition. Both are called, on their title-pages, the second edition. One was printed in Newburyport; the other probably in Salem. The author frequently addresses "mister printer," but nowhere in the copies which I have been able to trace (in five different libraries) is there the famous note about punctuation,—Dexter's one great contribution to eccentric literature. This note has been attributed almost invariably to the *second* edition of the "Pickle," but a considerable search and inquiry has failed to discover it in print earlier than 1838, or thirty-two years after Dexter had died.

The next edition, which I have found, is this one of 1838. It has forty-two pages, with an introductory essay "on His Life and Genius" and explanatory notes by "Peter Quince." I wish I knew who this Peter Quince might be. He has been confused with Isaac Story, Jr., who had previously used the same pseudonym, but died in 1803. This edition was printed and published in

Boston, and has a colored wrapper with a quaint picture of Dexter and his dog, derived from Akin's engraving. On page 42 occurs the celebrated note, definitely stated to be from the second edition:

[Note to Dexter's Second Edition]

fourder mister printer the Nowing ones complane of my book the fust edition had no stops I put in A nuf here and they may peper and solt it as they please

```
, , , , , , , , , , , , , , , , , , , , , , , , , , , , , , , , , , , , , , , , , , , , , , , , , , , ,
, , , , , , , , , , , , , , , , , , , , , , , , , , , , , , , , , , , , , , , , , , , , , , , , , , , ,
, , , , , , , , , , , , , , , , , , , , , , , , , , , , , , , , , , , , , , , , , , , , , , , , , , , ,
; ; ; ; ; ; ; ; ; ; ; ; ; ; ; ; ; ; ; ; ; ; ; ; ; ; ; ; ; ; ; ; ; ; ; ; ; ; ; ; ; ; ; ; ; ; ; ; ; ;
; ; ; ; ; ; ; ; ; ; ; ; ; ; ; ; ; ; ; ; ; ; ; ; ; ; ; ; ; ; ; ; ; ; ; ; ; ; ; ; ; ; ; ; ; ; ; ; ; ;
: : : : : : : : : : : : : : : : : : : : : : : : : : : : : : : : : : : : : : : : : : : : : : : : : : :
. . . . . . . . . . . . . . . . . . . . . . . . . . . . . . . . . . . . . . . . . . . . . . . . . . .
. . . . . . . . . . . . . . ! ! ! ! ! ! ! ! ! ! ! ! ! ! ! ! ! ! ! ! . . . . . . . . . . . . . . .
. . . . . . . . . . . . . . . . ! ! ! ! ! ! ! ! ! ! ! ! ! ! ! . . . . . . . . . . . . . . . .
. . . . . . . . . . . . . . . . . ! ! ! ! ! ! ! ! ! ! . . . . . . . . . . . . . . . . .
. . . . . . . . . . . . . . . . . . . . ! . . . . . . . . . . . . . . . . . . . . .
, , , , , , , , , , , , , , , , , , , , , , , , , , , , , , , , , , , , , , , , , , , , , , , , , , , ,
. . . . . . . . . . . ? ? ? ? ? ? ? ? ? ? ? ? ? ? ? ? . . . . . . . . . . . .
```

This Peter Quince edition had perhaps been suggested by a life of Dexter which had appeared in the same year. Samuel L. Knapp (who had written many biographical and other works) published his "Life of Timothy Dexter" in the year of his own death, 1838. He was able to include personal recollections of the man. He said that the "Pickle" was then out of print and even after "most diligent search," he could not get a copy. He does not discriminate between editions, nor even say that there ever was a second, but speaking of the punctuation marks, says that Dexter "put them all in the last

13

FROM THE MUSEUM OF

TIMOTHY DEXTER, Esq.

IME the firſt Lord in the younited States of A
mercary Now of Newburyport it is the voiſe of
the peopel and I cant Help it and ſo Let it goue Now
as I muſt be Lord there will ſoler many more Lords
prittey ſoune for it Dont hurt A Cat Nor the mouſe
Nor the ſon Nor the water Nor the Eare then goue
on all is Eaſey Now bons broaken all is well all in
Love Now I be gin to Lay the Corner ſton and the
kee ſton with grat Remenbrence of my father Jorge
Waſhington the grate herow 17 ſentreys paſt before
we found ſo good A father to his ſhildren and Now
gone to Reſt Now to ſhoue my Love to my father and
gaate Cariéters I will ſhoue the world one of the grate
Wonders of the world in 15 months if now man mour-
ders me in Dors or out Dors ſuch A mouſerum on
Earth will annonce O Lord thou knoweſt to be troue
ſourder hear me good Lord I am A goueing to Let or
ſhildren know Now to ſee good Lord what has bin in
the world grat wale back to owr ſore fathers Not old
plimeth but ſtop to Addom & Eave to ſhoue 45 fig-
ers two Leged and ſore Leged becoſe we Cant Doue
weel with out ſore Legd in the firſt plaſe they are our
ſoude in the Next plate to make out Dexters mouſeum
I wants 4 Lions to defend thous grat and miſtry men
from Eaſt to wiſt from North to South which Now
are at the plaſes Raſed the Lam is Not Readey in ſhort
meater if Agreabel I forme A good and peaſabel gov-
ement on my Land in Newburyport Compleat I take
3 preſedents hamſher govener all to Noue york and
the grate miſter John Jay is one, that maks 2 in that

From First Edition of the "Pickle"

page, requesting the reader to place them where he pleased." Knapp also says that the work contained a portrait of Dexter and his little dog, admirable likenesses. This reference, apparently to Akin's engraving, may indicate a confused state of Knapp's recollections ,of the "Pickle," or may pertain to some vanished edition.

The 1847, Newburyport, "Revised Edition" is expurgated, headings are introduced, and the text is rearranged by some editor. Punctuation is also introduced (by the editor) *in the text*, but there is no addendum with punctuation marks, and no reference to any such addition in any other editions. The preface says merely that Dexter's "style, manner, orthography and punctuation are entirely *original;* so far from purloining his material, Lord Dexter has even spelt and pointed in a way that no others have." The preface adds that "a proper punctuation" has been introduced, which detracts from "the originality of the work," but furnishes a key to the sense.

The preface to the Newburyport edition of 1848 says that the addendum covered a whole page of the second edition, and thus reprints it, without giving the sentence beginning "fourder mister printer." A reprint at the end of the third (1858) edition of Knapp's biography improves upon the version in the Peter Quince edition by adding to the marks, as they have been copied earlier in this chapter, another whole page of marks and signs: asterisks, daggers, double daggers, brackets, and paragraph marks,—thus painting the lily to death. The pamphlet has been reprinted a number of times since 1858. There is a reprint of the 1838 edition, dated

Boston, 1881; while the Historical Society of Old Newbury reprinted the same edition in 1916. Between 1881
and 1916, there was probably at least one other reprint.

Now, Dexter's whimsical conceit about punctuation
is the one thing by which he is known to hundreds of
book-collectors. Many persons who do not even recall
his name, have heard that there was once a curious old
man who wrote a book, omitted all punctuation, but put
dozens of periods and commas on the last page of a later
edition, and bade his readers "pepper and salt" the book
to their own taste.*

There is, in Appleton's "Cyclopedia of American Biography" (article Dexter) a dubious reference to this subject. It says: ". . . he published . . . 'A Pickle for the
Knowing Ones' and having been annoyed by the printers
about punctuation, he retaliated by writing a pamphlet
without a point of any kind, and at the end filled half
a page with points in a mass, inviting the readers to
'pepper the dish to suit themselves.' "

Two or three seeming inaccuracies occur in this sentence, especially the implication that there was another
pamphlet (not the "Pickle"), which nobody else has
ever mentioned.

No one can become even slightly familiar with Dexter's peculiarities without being convinced that the note
about the punctuation marks probably originated with
him. It is characteristic. Dexter is known to have been
a persistent writer of letters to the press,—could this

---

* Mrs. E. Vale Smith's "History of Newburyport" (1854) says that
Dexter "had several pages of punctuation marks printed separately, and
bound with the book."

ftate the king of grat britton mifter pitt Roufus king
Cros over to france Loues the 16 and then the grate
bonnepartey the grate and there fegnetoure Crow bid-
dey—I Command peafe and the grateft brotherly Love
and Not fade be Linked to gether with that beft of
troue Love fo as to govern all nafions on the fais of
the gloub not to tiranize over them but to put them
to order if any Defpout fhall A Rife as to boundreys
or Any maturs of Importence it is Left france and
grat britton and Amacarey to be fetteled A Congrefs
to be allways in france all Defpouts is to be thare fetteled and this may be Dun this will ballefs power and
then all wars Dun A way there-fore I have the Lam
to Lay Dow with the Lion Now this may be Dun if
thos three powers would A getay to Lay what is called Devel one fide and Not Carry the gentelman pack
hors Any longer but fhake him of as duft on your
feet and Laff at him ; there is grate noife Aboute a
toue Leged Creter he fays I am going to fet fade black
Divel there, ftop he would fcare the womans fo there
would be No youfe for the bilding, I fhould have to
E rect fum Noue won, Now I ftop hear, I puts the
Devil Long with the bull for he is a bulling 2 Leged
Annemal ftop put him one fide Near Soloman, Looking with Soloman to Ladey venus Now ftop wind up,
there is grat ods in froute I will Let you know the
fekret houe you may fee the Devel, ftand on your
head before a Loucking glafs and take a bibel in to
your boufum faft 40 owers and look in the loucking
glafs, there is no Devil if you dont fee the ould fellow,
but I affirm you will fee that old Devel
 Unto you all mankind Com to my heus to mock
and fneare whi ye Dont you Lafe be fore god or I

Dexter on International Peace.

note have taken the form of a newspaper communication? Or was it discussed by himself and his associates, but never printed until he was dead? Submitting these questions to three men, as learned in early American bibliography as any living—Messrs. Wilberforce Eames, Charles Evans, and George Parker Winship—I find them agreed in thinking that the note was probably really printed by his authority and in his life-time, but in some form not easily discoverable today. Mr. Eames suggests a missing edition of the "Pickle"; Mr. Evans, a broadside; Mr. Winship, a loose leaf to be inserted in the pamphlet.

It is always better to establish the truth of a pleasant legend than try to upset it. So in the hope that this may be read by someone who can supply the answers, I will end this chapter with three questions. Why did nearly all of Dexter's biographers assert that the note, with the punctuation marks, was in some edition of the "Pickle" (they usually specify the *second*) published in his life-time? (Dexter has been the subject of other works besides Knapp's biography,—articles in magazines and contributions to the transactions of historical societies.) Is there in existence any publication issued before October 1806, with this note to the printer? If not, does the note appear in print earlier than 1838?

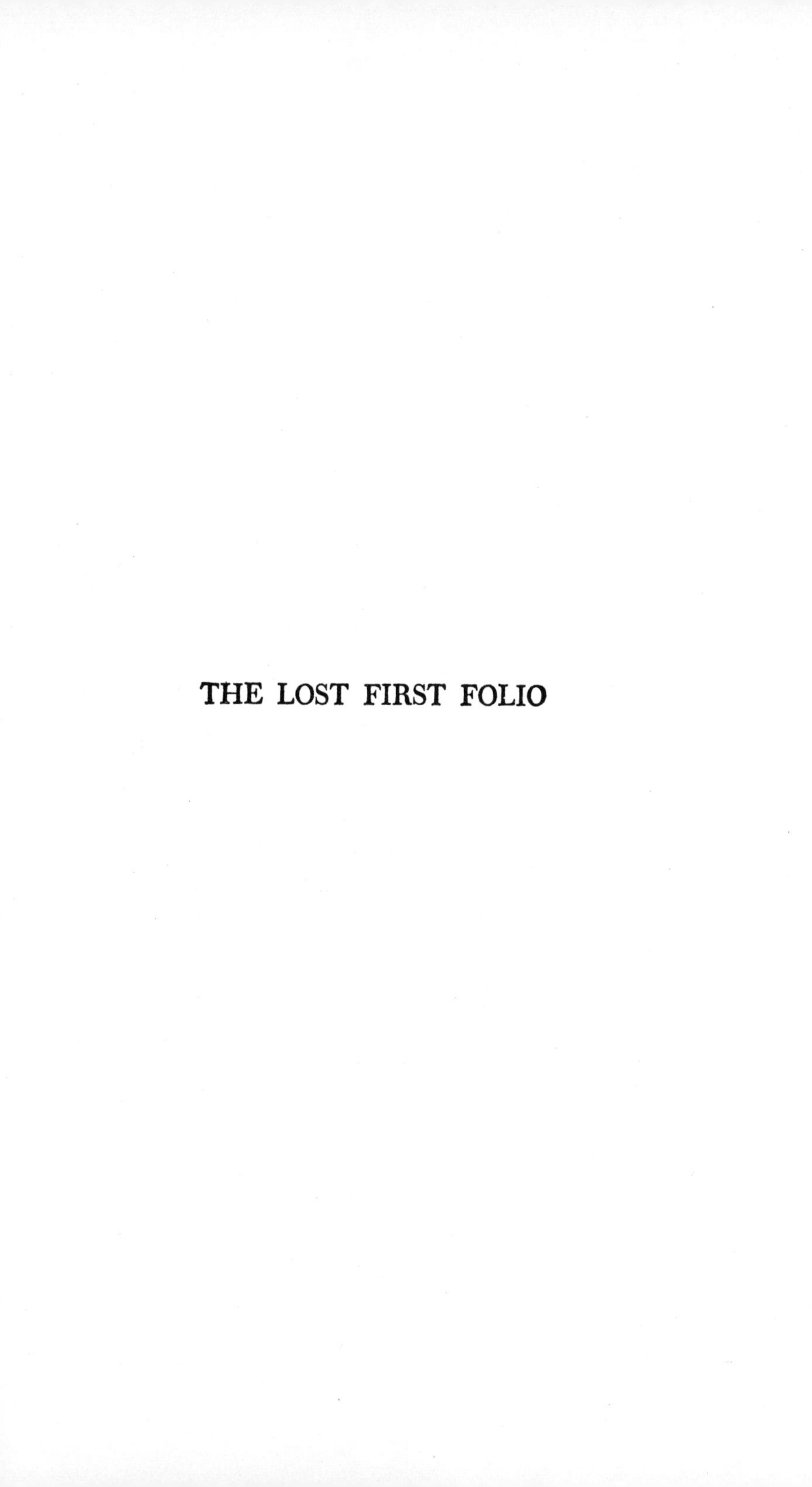

THE LOST FIRST FOLIO

CHAPTER XI

The sudden death of Mr. Agamemnon Jackson, and the story of his aunt's First Folio Shakespeare, are described by permission of Mr. Jackson himself. He expressed to me, in writing, only three days before his tragic decease, leave to print the correspondence, and the entries in his journal bearing on the incident. He passed away in a fit, on March 7th last. His landlady found a package of papers, some of which were addressed to me. She forwarded them, and I now print the record, with a few omissions.

Mr. Jackson did not usually sign more than the initial of his first name. He was not proud of the heroic style by which his parents adorned him. On one occasion, when he called upon me, I pointed out that there had been modern Agamemnons—there was one in the "Peterkin Papers," for instance. But it did not impress Mr. Jackson. I doubt if he ever read the "Peterkin Papers"— but of course I didn't say so. You never ask a book-collector if he has read a book. He is supposed to have read everything "*ex propria vigore*, as Hogan says." If you collect rare editions you have found the royal road to learning—or the reputation for learning. No one would be so silly as to ask a man who has just paid two hundred dollars for an early edition of Gray if he really cares anything about Gray.

Mr. Jackson, then, was known as A. Jackson. He came

into our library every few weeks to consult "Book Prices Current" or some of the other auction records. He never looked at other books. But I am sorry I shall see him no more. Let the letters and the diary relate the sorrowful story. The first is from his aunt, Mrs. Buxton:

Raspberry, Maine.

DEAR AGAMEMNON—I have not heard from you for nearly two months, although I can't find your letter, I think it must be at least two months ago, for I was just finishing the last of two dozen jars of damsons, which I put up for Mrs. Fessenden, who is living with me this winter, as she likes damsons, although I cannot say that I care very much for them myself, but they do very well for tea on Sundays. Your uncle never cared for them either, he and I agreed about that, as we did about pop-overs. Speaking about pop-overs reminds me—I am very much worried about my stock in that railroad—do you think that I had better sell it? We had pop-overs for tea—although as I say, I don't care for them myself—the same evening that Mr. Huff was here, you know he is cashier of the bank, and he said that although he made it a rule not to give advice about such things he thought I had better keep the stock for a while and see what happened, though it makes me nervous to read the papers nowadays, but what do you think?

Mrs. Fessenden is quite poorly. She says she remembers you very well when you came here one summer. You could not have been more than ten or twelve, it was the year before Blaine was nominated I think, when old Deacon Bradley married his second wife, she that was Hattie Trefethen and dyed his beard so as to look young and it all turned bright green, there was something the matter with the dye, they said. If you think I had better sell them, please let me know, won't you.

With much love,
AUNT MARTHA.

P.S.—There are a lot of old books in that box of your uncle's in the garret. Do you want them? I will send them to you if you do, for what with papers and the magazines, I don't want any more books than those we have in the book-case in the parlor now. You remember what a great reader your uncle was. And he was executor of Dr. Perley's estate—and part of the books came to him by the will. You wouldn't recall old Dr. Perley—his wife was a perfect martyr, I always said, and kept everything going while he was gali-vanting about Europe buying more books than he ever could read. Besides, Mrs. Fessenden's niece who is a teacher in the High School, brings home books all the time from the library. So you can have them if you want them. I'll get old Dave Lunt to pack them up.

Mr. Jackson's reply, of which he kept a copy, was as follows:

DEAR AUNT MARTHA—I was glad to hear from you, and I hope that your health is still good. It would be very unwise, from all that I hear, for you to sell that stock. In order to be sure, however, I will ask a man I know who follows these things more closely than I do, what his opinion is about it. Then I will be able to advise you. Please give my regards to Mrs. Fessenden. I do not seem to remember her—but, of course, I wouldn't say that to her. Thank you for the offer of the books—I could tell better about them if you would let me know their titles.

Always affectionately your nephew,
A. JACKSON.

On the bottom of the sheet Mr. Jackson had later added a note:

I wrote that last sentence, inquiring about the books, merely to be polite. Jackass!

His aunt's reply:

Raspberry, Maine.

DEAR AGAMEMNON—I am surprised you don't remember Mrs. Fessenden, and she seemed to feel quite bad when I

told her you had forgotten all about her. She says she
saved you from a whipping once when you brought a pail
full of eels and bullfrogs into the house, and one of the
frogs jumped right into a bowl of dough where your grandmother was making marble cake. She says for me to ask
if you don't remember the time you fell into the pig-pen
and she pulled you out. Of course I will sell the stock if
you really think I had better, though Mr. Huff says he
thinks I better keep it. I hope you won't get the grip; most
everyone has got it this winter, and old Mrs. Buntin is real
sick. Just think, she was ninety-seven the tenth of last
September.

With much love,
Aunt Martha.

P.S.—I got Miss Peavey, Mrs. Fessenden's niece, to copy
down the names of the books, she's real smart and knows all
about books and worked in the library one summer, while
Miss Damon went on a vacation down to Peak's Island.

The list was enclosed. Here is a copy of it.

1. Wide, Wide World, The.
2. Hannibal Hamlin, Life of.
3. Among the Cannibals.
4. One Thousand Useful Facts.
5. Satan in Society.
6. The Dying Unitarian, or Never Too Late to Seek God's
   Mercy.
7. Indian Dream-book, The.
8. Shakespeare's Comedies, &c.
9. Complete Horse Doctor, The.
10. Noted Men of Cumberland County.
11. The Gin Drinker's Grave.
12. The Spy, by Jas. Fenimore Cooper.
13. Darkness and Daylight in New York.
14. Earth, Sea and Sky, or, The Wonders of the Universe.
15. Friendship's Casket.

Entry from Mr. Jackson's diary: "I should never have
paid any more attention to this preposterous lot of rub-

bish, if Miss Peavey or whatever her name was, had not written on the edge of the list, near 'Shakespeare's Comedies' the words: 'This looks *very* old.' So when I wrote to Aunt Martha, thanking her for her trouble, and saying that I didn't believe I cared for any of the books, I added this: 'Please ask Miss Peavey how old the Shakespeare is.'"

This is Mrs. Buxton's reply:

Raspberry, Maine.

DEAR AGAMEMNON—I would have asked Miss Peavey about the book but she has gone to stay with her cousin's wife in Sacarappa for a month, as her youngest baby is only eight weeks old and the hired girl has left and so everything is all upset. They are real nice people, her husband owns one of the biggest grocery stores in Sacarappa. They call it Westbrook, or something, now, but it is always Sacarappa to me. What is the use of being stuck-up? It's just because the negro minstrel folks made so much fun of the name Sacarappa. Suppose they did. Your uncle's brother lived there for over twenty years until he joined the New Jerusalemiters or whatever they call themselves, and went careering about the world with that crazy creature, and got wrecked on the coast of Africa in a hurricane, and came back looking like a skeleton, with two front teeth knocked out somehow. He got some false ones made up in Augusta and they didn't fit him, and he sued the man and they were still fighting over it when I heard last. Good-bye and be sure to take care of yourself when you go out.

With much love,

AUNT MARTHA.

P.S.—It was the "Life of Hannibal Hamlin" you asked about, wasn't it? Shall I send it to you?

DEAR AUNT MARTHA—Do not send the "Life of Hannibal Hamlin." The book I asked about was the Shakespeare, but it is of no consequence at all. Do not bother any more in the matter.

Affectionately yours,
A. JACKSON.

Raspberry, Maine.

DEAR AGAMEMNON—Why didn't you say before that it was the Shakespeare book you wanted to know about? I had to go up into the garret this morning to get an extra quilt for Mrs. Fessenden's bed, for she is always complaining about being cold, though it seems to me that if she ate more sensible food instead of those things made out of straw and bran that she buys for her health instead of good meat and vegetables her blood wouldn't be so thin. But she went to a place out in Indiana, where they eat nothing but grain, and learned all this foolishness. I brought down the Shakespeare book and Mrs. Fessenden is reading it now, but she says that all those s's that look like f's make her feel as if her mouth was full of cotton-batting, and it's too bad Shakespeare didn't get his books printed at the Bangor Times Job Printing Office, because they would have done it much better. I must say that if Shakespeare looked like that picture—if it's meant to be him—he was no beauty. His head looks like a gourd. Old Mrs. Buntin died Saturday. They say she left all her property to her niece's folks, and cut off her own great-grandson without a cent.

With much love,
AUNT MARTHA.

Entry in Mr. Jackson's diary: "Head like a gourd! My God! the Droeshout portrait."

DEAR AUNT MARTHA: Will you look at that Shakespeare again, and tell me these things?

1. Is the portrait of Shakespeare on the title-page itself— that is, is it on the page where the name of the book is given?

Mr. WILLIAM
SHAKESPEARES

COMEDIES,
HISTORIES, &
TRAGEDIES.

Published according to the True Originall Copies.

LONDON
Printed by Isaac Iaggard, and Ed. Blount. 1623

2. What is the date of the book? Look at the bottom of
   the title-page for this.
3. What else does it say at the bottom of the title-page?
                                Yours in great haste.
                                       A. JACKSON.

Answer to the foregoing:

Raspberry, Maine.

DEAR AGAMEMNON—Before I forget it I want to ask you
if you will go to the *Congregationalist Observer* office and
ask them why I didn't get my last number. Tell them I
have subscribed ever since 1868, and that I have always
paid the subscription as regular as the bill came around,
but I didn't get my number today, and I thought they ought
to know about it. I don't like to think there is anyone dis-
honest in our post office here, though of course that may be
it, for there's a new man who hasn't been in Raspberry but
about four years and he came from Chicago although he
looks honest. But if you will go in and see, why they can
tell you if they sent it. That was all wrong about old Mrs.
Buntin's will. Her great-grandson, you remember him,
don't you? He went to Bowdoin College one year, but
now he's home, and they say he smokes cigarettes, gets the
sawmill, and twelve hundred dollars.
                                With much love,
                                    AUNT MARTHA.

Scrawled on the bottom of this letter, in Mr. Jackson's
handwriting: "Suffering Cats! was there ever such a
woman!"

DEAR AUNT MARTHA—Will you please answer the questions about the Shakespeare I asked in my letter?
                                In haste,
                                     A. JACKSON.

Raspberry, Maine.

DEAR AGAMEMNON—I dropped your letter in the hall upstairs and Mrs. Fessenden found it and thought it was just a scrap of paper and wiped her curling-irons on it. But I found it in her waste basket—and that reminds me you needn't trouble about the *Observer*, for it came all right on Monday. I'm glad to know that that young man in the post office didn't take it.

With much love,
AUNT MARTHA.

P.S.—Yes, the picture is on the page you speak of. It is a big one, and he looks as if he needed a shave. The date is 1623. Just think of that!

It says at the bottom—London. Printed by Isaac Iaggard (That's what it looks like, anyhow) and Ed. Blount. I knew an Ed. Blunt once—he was your uncle's hired man when we lived in Kittery.

Telegram

MRS. MARTHA BUXTON, Raspberry, Me.—Is there a poem opposite title-page ? Wire reply collect.

A. JACKSON.

Raspberry, Maine.

DEAR AGAMEMNON—Well, you certainly gave us all a turn with your telegram. Mrs. Fessenden saw the boy coming up the path with that yellow envelope and she sank back on the sofa and sat right down on my work-basket and might have got lock-jaw from sitting on my button-hole scissors. She said she knew something had happened to her sister in Dover whose house was broken into last fall by two Italians who got into a fight next day and one of them nearly killed the other one and she had to go down and be a witness in court. As for me all I could think of was the last time a telegram came into this house when your uncle broke his leg down to Camden on an excursion with the Odd Fellows, and when he was being brought home some

Meddlesome Matty or other gave him a drink of liquor, which went right to his head because he was not used to it, so when they brought him into the house he was singing an awful song about Terrar rar boom Derray or something, with the minister right here and everybody. I thought I could never look them in the face again. However I was glad it was nothing worse, and after I went upstairs and got Mrs. Fessenden's bottle of cologne in case it was bad news about her sister, and I had to rub her head, we opened the telegram. Well, I don't see what there is to be so excited about, but then you know about these books and I don't. Yes, there is a kind of a thing that looks like a poem on the page across from the picture, but it is awful poor poetry. I hope you are taking care of yourself. Don't get your feet wet.

With much love,
AUNT MARTHA.

The next is a letter, by special delivery from Mr. Jackson.

DEAR AUNT MARTHA—I am very sorry I frightened you with the telegram, but I am very much interested in that book. Does the poem begin with the words *To the Reader* and is it signed *B.I.*?

Affectionately yours,
A. JACKSON.

Raspberry, Maine.

DEAR AGAMEMNON—I got your special delivery letter last night when I went down to the post office which you know is in Carr's grocery. Jeff Carr said that if the folks in Washington expect him to go traipsing all round town with letters just because somebody has stuck a blue stamp on them, they will have to get him another boy, for his hired man was out taking some eggs to Dr. Roberts who is sick himself and eats twelve eggs a day, so everybody says. Yes, the poem begins and ends just the way you wrote. Little Nat Batchelder was here last night, he is Mrs. Fessenden's niece Lottie's second boy, and he wanted to take the book to school to show the teacher and the children, because it is so old, and he is going to speak a piece from Shakespeare next Saturday, something from Julius Cæsar, but I wouldn't let him take it because I was afraid he might hurt it. He felt real bad, and I was sorry afterwards, and I thought I'd tell him tomorrow that if he would *promise* to take *good care* of it, he might have it. You don't tell me anything about yourself. Are you all right?

With much love,
Aunt Martha.

Comment scrawled on the margin of the foregoing, in a shaky hand, by Mr. Jackson: "Letting a kid take a First Folio to school with him! *Good Lord!*" The rest is not decipherable. Mr. Jackson's pen made some more marks, but his emotion was too great, and they are illegible.

Telegram—Night letter

Mrs. Martha Buxton, Raspberry, Me.—Take care of that book. Don't let anyone get it. Don't let anyone read it. Don't let anyone hurt it. Am coming up to see it as soon as I can get out of bed. Have got grippe. Put it in the bank if you can. Above all, say nothing about it to anyone.

A. Jackson.

Raspberry, Maine.

Dear Agamemnon—Your long telegram, which came this morning, frightened us most to death. I hope your illness has not made you delirious. You need not worry about the book—it is all right and no one shall harm it. In fact Mrs. Fessenden has been quite interested in it, and she found a real nice picture of Shakespeare in an old copy of *Harper's Bazar,* which she cut out, and then she cut out that awful thing in the book, and burned it up and pasted the new one in. So you see the book will be ever so much improved. What are you doing for your grip? Mr. Fassett, next door, had it and he drank a cup of anise-seed tea every night and he says it did him lots of good. You better try it.

With much love,
AUNT MARTHA.

The nurse who was attending Mr. Jackson tells me that he scarcely moaned after reading this letter. He had one quick convulsion, and then it was all over.

WITH ACKNOWLEDGEMENTS TO THOMAS
DE QUINCEY

CHAPTER XII

That stroke of genius in which De Quincey conceived the title, "On Murder considered as one of the Fine Arts," compelled the attention of his contemporaries, and ensured that for a century to come, everybody who could read English should at least have heard of his essay.

Genius has a fashion of being much more vivid than the self-styled and self-conscious Moderns; the groups and schools which plume themselves on their audacity usually achieve nothing but a pale copy. The irony, the grim humor with which De Quincey reported the proceedings of his Society of Connoisseurs in Murder set its mark upon the literature of crime; a reflection of it is to be found, for instance, in Mr. Charles Whibley's "Book of Scoundrels."

At his best De Quincey is inimitable. In the section which discusses various philosophers who were murdered —or nearly murdered—he comes to Hobbes. This is his opening remark: "Hobbes—but why, or on what principle, I never could understand—was not murdered." And there is the matchless passage in which the author shows how dangerous it is for a man to indulge himself in murder, because he may go on to robbery, and thence to drinking and Sabbath-breaking, and from that to incivility and procrastination. This paragraph ends with the observation: "Many a man has dated his ruin from some murder or other that perhaps he thought little of at the time."

For a hundred who have heard the title of the essay, perhaps three have read it. If you ask for it at a book-shop, you may be offered that impediment to reading: a set of "Complete Works." Or the book-seller will vanish for a while, then return and tell you that he can sell you a copy of the "Opium Eater." As for the other, —"We can get it for you, Sir." Few read De Quincey nowadays, and the few are mostly students who are sent to one of his essays (not the one on Murder) in preparation for college examinations.

At first, De Quincey speaks merely of a number of brutal assassinations. When he commences to particu-larize, he commends the murder of Gustavus Adolphus for its unique quality, in that it occurred at noonday, and on the field of battle. He admits that the grand feature of mystery, in some shape or other "ought to colour every judicious attempt at murder." Yet he dis-approves of poisonings,—apparently on patriotic grounds. "Can they not keep to the old honest way of cutting throats, without introducing such abominable innova-tions from Italy?" This recalls the plaint of the Ameri-can legislator who was opposing a bill to adopt the electric chair for inflicting the death penalty: "I am against it, Mr. Speaker! Hanging was good enough for my grandfather, and it's good enough for me!" The denunciation of the poisoners is in that section of the essay which appeared in 1827; in his later years he had come perhaps to a sounder opinion. His biographer, Mr. Masson, says that he paid a great amount of attention to "the trial of Palmer in 1856 and to another famous case in 1857." Now, Palmer was, of course, a poisoner; while, as any amateur in murder will instantly tell you, 1857 is memorable for a murder and a trial which not only dwarfed all others of that year, but set a standard forever. Of all the reputed followers of Lucretia Borgia, Miss Madeleine Smith is eminent, not only for her winsome personality, but for the very pretty problem she set a number of citizens, advocates and judges, of her day, and the murder-fancier forever.

The foundation of De Quincey's essay seems to be the barbarous killing of two families by one John Williams in London in 1811. There is a strong element of terror in the crimes, because about twelve days separated the attacks on the two families, and the first had spread so much fear abroad that the public mind was already excited and horrified when the second blow fell. There is also some mystery. De Quincey accepts the guilt of Williams as undoubted; a later account which I have seen is less certain about it. Williams committed suicide in jail; and that, Daniel Webster would say, is confession. But while some of the evidence against Williams was very damaging, there was still room for doubt. The murderer spared neither man, woman nor child, and as no ordinary motive appeared for slaying these people, Williams, if guilty, must have been one of those hideous creatures who, like the weasel, sheds blood for the mere savage joy of it. In other words, he was a homicidal maniac, and the murders do not at all belong in the category of those to be considered by De Quincey. There was terror in them, and a little mystery; otherwise they were a senseless slaughter, and unworthy the attention paid them by his club of amateurs.

The greatest scholar among the men to whose teaching I have been privileged to listen is Professor George Lyman Kittredge. In his lectures on Shakespeare, naturally enough he had something to say about murder, and the mawkish attitude which some persons adopt toward it. In one of his books* he sums up his opinions:

Now, nothing is more interesting than Murder. Murder is the material of great literature,—the *raw* material, if you will, but is not raw material essential to production, as well in art as in manufactures? What distinguishes De Quincey's famous Postscript on certain memorable murders from the grewsome scareheaded "stories" of the purveyor for the daily press? Surely not the matter! The bare plot of the sublimest of Greek tragedies, the Agamemnon of Æschylus, finds its closest parallel in a horrible butchery in low life that occurred in New York a few years ago. Conventional phrases are always tiresome enough, but none is more so than that of "morbid curiosity" as applied to the desire to know the circumstances of a great crime. The phrase is like a proverb: it is only half true, though it masquerades as one of the eternal verities. Curiosity is natural; without it a man is a mere block, incapable of intellectual advancement. And curiosity about crime and criminals is no less natural, no further morbid—that is, diseased or abnormal—than that which attaches to any other startling event or remarkable personage. Like all other forms of curiosity, it may *become* morbid, and perhaps it is well to restrain it,—but that is not the question.

The interest in murder is shared by practically everyone, except a few who think the subject is "low" or degrading. There are also the gentlemen who have

* "The Old Farmer and his Almanack."

acquired a reputation for exquisite literary taste by decrying every author in the world except, perhaps, one, and every subject for literature except one. The single author whom they praise is invariably a European, and usually a Frenchman. His devotees are condemned to the perusal of a monotonous catalogue of adulteries. The idea that the infraction of one commandment alone is the sole topic for literature is a curious example of the bigotry which, with some folk, accompanies vociferous demands for literary freedom. It is an odd notion which discerns freedom in ossification.

Murder is not a topic foreign to any of us. One does not have to be a police officer, nor an assistant district attorney, like Mr. Arthur Train, to whom a prosecution for murder is a matter of routine, to realize that the subject is near at hand. James Payn is quoted as hazarding a guess that one person in every five hundred is an undiscovered murderer. "This," says H. B. Irving, with decided gusto, "gives us all a hope, almost a certainty, that we may reckon one such person at least among our acquaintances." Mr. Irving adds that he was one of three men discussing this subject in a London club. They were able to name six persons of their various acquaintance who were, or had been, suspected of being successful murderers.

Probably most men, and some women, could, if they would, give similar testimony. A member of my family actually witnessed a murder; and this in no lawless community, but on a quiet street of a city. Inside a period of less than four years it happened, even to as cloistered a person as myself, to take part in two trials for murder, once as member of a court martial, and in a civil trial as foreman of the jury. A number of years earlier I had a curious experience in a museum connected with a university. It was late in the afternoon, just before closing time, and I was hunting for some specimen which I wished to see. Down the long aisle of the museum there came hurrying a gentleman, putting on his hat and coat,—evidently one of the museum staff, leaving for the day. He stopped, however, when he saw that I was looking for something, and asked, most politely, if he could be of any assistance. I explained what it was I was trying to find, and he led me to another room, and took pains to show me the specimen, which I think was a bird of some kind. After giving me further information about it, and saying good-night with more than ordinary courtesy, he departed, leaving me interested, not in the bird, but in his own identity. His face was familiar; I had certainly seen him before, and under such peculiar circumstances that I felt the utmost curiosity to remember why he had made such an impression. After torturing myself for half an hour, I recollected the polite gentleman: I had seen him only once before, but that was in court, where he was on trial for his life, on the charge of murder.

No specialist in murder should miss the precepts formed by Miss Carolyn Wells in "The Technique of the Mystery Story," about the most amusing volume ever found masquerading as a text-book. One is this: "A true lover of detective fiction never reads detailed newspaper accounts of crime." In conversation Miss Wells readily admits exceptions to this statement, citing the Elwell murder,—which certainly might have been planned and executed by a devotee of Mrs. Anna Katharine Green's novels. On a later page Miss Wells declares that the theory upon which Stevenson and Lloyd Osbourne built their murder and mystery story "The Wrecker," is quite wrong, inasmuch as a mystery story cannot be combined with a novel of manners.

It is dangerous to try to define the true lover of detective fiction. It would be surprising to learn that De Quincey was not a true lover of such detective fiction as was available in his day. He wrote some of it; and he certainly read newspaper accounts of crime. Is not Sir Arthur Conan Doyle a lover of detective fiction? He has concerned himself with the actual cases of Edalji and of Oscar Slater in his own country, and while in New York in 1914 sought an interview with Charles Becker, then under sentence of death. I would praise far more than does Miss Wells, in her book, Arthur Train's "True Stories of Crime"; if half of the books of detective fiction were as entertaining as Mr. Train's narratives there would be more interesting reading in the world. "The Wrecker" is truly, for its lack of form, more open to criticism than anything else by Stevenson. But as a mystery story, about people in whom the reader is made to feel an interest, and under circumstances so carefully described as to seem credible, it is like a mountain-peak rising high over the foot-hills of thousands of average detective tales. Sherlock Holmes once made a remark to the general effect that a detective mystery should be stated in as direct and simple terms as a theorem of Euclid. Not pausing to notice that this is Holmes' remark, and not that of his creator, a number of writers have gone to wreck upon this theory,—just as others have blamed Sir Arthur Conan Doyle for jeering at Poe's Dupin, when it was really Holmes who jeered. If the author of the Sherlock Holmes stories had carried out this Euclid plan, we should never have heard of Holmes.

To collect murders requires care, taste, and judgment, as with anything else. To amass an indiscriminate heap of orchids, of Italian rapiers, or of opals, with no criterion except the utterly absurd one, say, of size, is to fill your house with rubbish. The great gallery of distinguished murderers has no room for a horde of rough-and-tumble slayers. De Quincey, in truth, noted this fact when he wrote that "something more goes to the composition of a fine murder than two blockheads to kill and be killed—a knife—a purse—and a dark lane." And again, he condemns "old women and the mob of newspaper readers" who are "pleased with anything provided it is bloody enough." The subject of a murder, he says, ought to be a good man, he should not be a public character, and he ought to be in good health,—"for it is absolutely barbarous to murder a sick person, who is usually quite unable to bear it." As to "the time, the place, and the tools," he adds that the good sense of the practitioner "has usually directed him to night and privacy." He notes an exception,—a murder to which I shall refer later.

Can we take these principles as they were laid down by De Quincey, and while admitting their importance to all fanciers of murder, try to revise them in the light of later research? Is it possible thereby to raise some standards for today to which the collectors of murders may repair? How, in short, do we define the *pure murder*, —not as the scientific criminologist uses the term, but as the collector and amateur may be permitted to employ it?

First, it is necessary to eliminate, to exclude, to state what kind of killings are not *pure murders*. The rule against the murder of public characters is sound, as everyone will agree. The political assassination has too many other aspects aside from the destruction of the individual; the whole matter is confused, hopelessly, with issues which have nothing to do with the problem of murder.

Next, and this is an extremely important, although difficult, point, the *crime passionel* is, generally speaking, to be ruled out. The jealous lover, the forsaken maiden, the injured husband, the discarded mistress, the vengeful wife,—these stock characters in the melodrama of life are forever killing somebody or other, but there is in their deeds an extraneous and even sensational interest, which detracts from its value in the eyes of the austere amateur of murder. Their crimes are, with rare exceptions, so excessively cheap,—the stuff for the Sunday supplement in the yellow press. The folk who dote upon them,—vulgarians and riff-raff.

A love affair, licit or otherwise, may be interesting by itself; a murder is almost inevitably so. Combine the two, and, as with many mixtures (shandygaff, for example), you merely spoil both components. And there is a still higher ground for objection to the murder which has its origin in sexual passion: it is frequently so immoral. Touch pitch and be defiled!

Newspapermen pretend that the public will take no extended interest in any murder "unless there is a woman in it," and acting upon this belief, they sometimes do strange things. Not long ago it chanced to be my duty to become acquainted with the minutest details of a murder which had been committed twenty years earlier. The cause of the murder was a quarrel over the price of meat,—that and nothing else. Yet when the investigation was over, and I had the curiosity to look at the old newspaper reports of the crime, the very first one I discovered referred to a "dark-eyed and beautiful brunette," evolved out of the inner consciousness of some faithful reporter. She, according to his story written on the day of the murder, had urged the slayer to his dreadful deed. No mention whatever was made of the true cause: the prosaic bacon and sausages.

Yet it must be admitted that to make this rule absolute, to deny any fascination whatever to those murders which spring from love and jealousy would be a serious blunder. The exception to a rule may be brilliant and it is in this instance. Since the day, nearly seventy years ago, when Miss Madeleine Smith, "her step as buoyant and her eyes as bright as if she were entering a box at the opera" took her place in the dock at Edinburgh, it has been impossible to dispose of the crime of passion as altogether unworthy of attention. Miss Smith, with her celebrated brown silk dress, her lavender gloves, and silver-topped smelling bottle, and it is murmured, her pretty foot and ankle displayed for the benefit of the judges, fixed the attention of the world upon that High Court of Justiciary for nine long days,—an incredible time for a trial in 1857. As the jury, by a majority of 13 to 2, decided that it was "not proven" that she had put arsenic in the cocoa or coffee with which she entertained her lover, M. Émile L'Angelier, it would probably be unwise to express the opinion that there was something peculiar about those drinks. It is not absolutely outside the bounds of human possibility that Miss Smith survives today,* the wife or the widow of one of those "hundreds of gentlemen" who wrote to her at the close of the trial, some of them offering her "consolation" and some "their hearts and homes." So if there were doubtful souls who resolutely declined to accept tea or coffee of her brewing, there were many others who scorned such ungallant suspicions. In his careful history of the trial, Mr. A. Duncan Smith names sixteen different books or pamphlets on the case, but later than any of

---

* Lord Riddell in a recent book implies that she died, a happy wife and mother, at the age of 80,—i.e., in about the year 1916. I think this is an error. A writer in *Notes and Queries* (Oct. 14, 1911) gives his authorities for the statement that she entered upon two marriages, neither of them fortunate, one with a Dr. Hora in 1857, and one with a Mr. Wardle (O, Pickwick!) in 1861. As Mrs. Wardle she died at Melbourne, Sept. 29, 1893.

these appeared a novel, "The House in Queen Anne Square" by W. D. Lyell, published about 1911. There is in this a fantastic resemblance to some of the facts in the Madeleine Smith case, none of them stranger than that the heroine appears as a most woefully persecuted and maligned virgin, of saintly character.

Mr. William Roughead, the admirable historian of Scottish murders and mysteries, relates in his book, "Twelve Scots Trials," the adventures of Mrs. John Gilmour (born Christina Cochran) who preceded Miss Smith by thirteen years. Uncharitable officers of the Crown professed to see a connection between certain purchases of arsenic by this lady and the subsequent death, under painful circumstances, of her newly married husband. Aided by her friends, Mrs. Gilmour found it discreet to retire to America; she arrived in New York about June 1843, and was thus an early member of that troop of pilgrims who come, not in battalions but as single spies, across the Atlantic. Oscar Slater and Dr. Crippen were known to our own time for their voyages hither. But the hand of the law rested not so heavily upon Christina Gilmour as upon these later fugitives.

Another kind of crime which is not within our field is the murder committed by a madman. I know that there is a current weakness for the saying: *"All* criminals are insane." But law, medicine, and religion alike know better; to say it, is a sign of that oily philanthropy which thinks it noble to express rosy opinions which everyone knows are untrue. It finds a similar manifestation in talking about the inmates of a prison as a lot of capital fellows who have been cruelly "misunderstood" by the folk outside; it expresses itself by showing the liveliest sympathy for all murderers of an especially barbarous type, but it never utters a word of regret for their victims. Those who form their opinions of the world and its people from observation, and not by viewing them through a mist of sentimentality, know that just as there are no limits to the heights of nobility and self-sacrifice of which human nature is capable, so there has never been found any measuring rod or line to sound the depths to which it can descend. When a crime is done and folk begin to say: "Oh, she (or he) could *never* have done anything so dreadful as that!" it would be well for them to know of Miss Constance Kent, a well-bred girl of sixteen, who in England, about 1860, took her infant half-brother out of the house in the middle of the night, and cut his throat,—merely to express her disapproval of step-mothers and second marriages.* She subsequently saw her father, and also a nurse, suspected of the crime, and left them to their fate,—which might have been the gallows, so far as she did anything to prevent it. It would also be well to recall "an American mother" (a phrase sometimes used as synonymous with innocence) named Mrs. Whiteling, who in Pennsylvania, in 1888, poisoned her husband, her daughter aged nine, and her son aged three, in order to collect their insurance,—a total sum of $399. Another useful

---

* A sentiment which, Mr. James L. Ford would say, was shared by the editor of the *New York Ledger*. See Chapter II of "The Literary Shop,"—the one published in 1894, not the later one of similar title. But, of course, Mr. Robert Bonner never translated his aversion to step-mothers into the line of conduct pursued by Miss Kent, the heroine of the Road Mystery.

memory is that of the Rev. Mr. Richeson, a clergyman actually in charge of a parish, who as he acquired the poison with which to kill the girl he had betrayed (and to clear the way for a marriage to a wealthier lady) accompanied the purchase with a remark of fiendish cynicism. The faction had already arisen* which "would never believe that he could do such a dreadful thing," when—he confessed.

The act of the genuine madman, however, usually has no place in a study of pure murder. It is not of interest, for the same reason that the tragedy of "Hamlet" would not be of interest if the hero were insane,—as some readers have professed to believe that he was. The most notorious crimes supposed to be the work of a maniac, are, of course, the Whitechapel murders in 1888. I refer to them only to cite the extraordinarily skilful novel by Mrs. Belloc Lowndes, called "The Lodger," which is based upon them. Of all the novels which I have read, with murder for their theme, I know of few better than this. Mrs. Lowndes has taken the most revolting crimes, and treated them unobjectionably; there is nothing in the book which need disturb any reader whose nerves are

---

* A situation of this kind is described in "Tom Sawyer." Injun Joe, after murdering a man, and getting another accused of it, is found dead, a fact which, Mark Twain writes, "stopped the further growth of one thing—the petition to the Governor for Injun Joe's pardon. The petition had been largely signed, many tearful and eloquent meetings had been held, and a committee of sappy women been appointed to go in deep mourning and wail around the Governor and implore him to be a merciful ass and trample his duty under foot. Injun Joe was believed to have killed five citizens of the village, but what of that? If he had been Satan himself there would have been plenty of weaklings ready to scribble their names to a pardon petition, and drip a tear on it from their permanently impaired and leaky water-works."

in proper order. And yet the effect of some of the passages is only surpassed (if they are surpassed) by such
great murder-chapters as Mr. Tulkinghorn's return to
his chambers in "Bleak House," and the interview with
the murderer in the lonely house, in Arthur Morrison's
"The Green Diamond."* "The Lodger" is an exception;
the art of its author has made a homicidal maniac interesting.

The murder accompanying a robbery is not a proper
subject for our collection, if it arises as a more or less
unpremeditated event. If it is planned as part and par-
cel of the robbery—and is not a mere incident thereto—
it may have excellent points. Such instances as those
of the numerous army of peddlers who were perpetually
getting murdered all over Europe during the Eighteenth
and Nineteenth Centuries are not to be despised. The
Polish Jew, in "The Bells," is a familiar example; almost
every country town had one of them. De Quincey cites
the Begbie Mystery (it is always honored with the capital
M) in Edinburgh in 1806, as a *daylight* murder. As
it took place about five o'clock of a November afternoon,
I doubt if there could have been much daylight lurking
about.† It was a bold and well-planned murder, as a
necessary prelude to a robbery. The murderer is still
unknown, and by this time, probably beyond reach of
the law. For an account of it, together with some plau-
sible suspicions, I must refer you again to Mr. Roughead; to his volume "The Riddle of the Ruthvens."

It is possible that, as a matter of strict principle, we

* Called in England, "The Green Eye of Goona."
† Walter Scott also says "broad daylight." Maybe I am wrong.

should exclude those persons with whom murder is not a master-stroke—brilliant, amazing, and above all, unique—but with whom it has become a morbid custom —an addiction. There will be objections to this, and some illustrious names will be cited in disproof. The world, careless as it is, has not yet forgotten M. Landru, who in 1922 suffered the extreme penalty of the law in the streets of Paris, for the murder of—was it *eleven* persons? The late H. B. Irving, one of the most distinguished of all collectors in this field, and author of three books which it is impossible to praise too highly, died before he could write of Landru. His ac- quaintance with French crime, and the manner of all his writings on this subject, show that he should have been Landru's historian. Mr. H. C. Bailey, the novelist, wrote a good essay on Landru for the *Daily Telegraph*. He did not fail to notice the peculiar humor of the prisoner,—a humor which charmed Paris for many weeks. From the beginning, M. Landru seems to have thought of himself as a man bound by all the considerations of chivalry to protect, from the vulgar prying of the police, the reputations of those who had confided to him their fortunes and their hearts. Officials were curious to dis- cover why so many ladies who retired to M. Landru's country homes never seemed to come back to Paris,— nor, indeed, to be found again anywhere. His answers were always in the same strain,—that of the gallant, high-minded gentleman. Where were Mme. Cuchet and her son? He declined to answer. "I have nothing to say. I have always said that the private affairs of Mme. Cuchet and her son were nobody's business." Why should she have vanished? "Here," said M. Landru, "we come to certain matters which I have *always* refused to reveal." What had become of Mme. Laborde-Line? "The private life of Mme. Laborde-Line," said he, "is a wall which I am not willing to scale. . . . I have had commercial transactions with women. It is not my business to know what became of the women." How about Mme. Guillin,—where is she? "As to her disappearance, I have nothing to say. It has taken four years to lay hands on me, for they have been looking for me since 1915, and only arrested me in 1919. They have only been looking for Mme. Guillin three years. Perhaps they will find her yet." He could be sardonic. On the last day of his trial, as he gazed at the women struggling for seats in the court, he was heard to murmur: "If any of those ladies would like my place I will very willingly give it up to them." No; M. Landru must not lightly be dismissed because, in his practice of murder, he seems to have been unable to observe moderation.

Similarly, England puts forward the claims of George Joseph Smith, who, about 1915, invested the commonplace bath-tub with a new element of romance by making this humble receptacle the scene of a succession of murders, in which the subjects, I regret to say, were all ladies. Perhaps, in employing a bath for the murder of these ladies, Mr. Smith felt that he was, in some fashion, avenging the male sex. His great exemplars in this method were both women: Clytemnestra and Charlotte Corday.

And our own country—never behind the other nations —offers, for the connoisseur, Herman W. Mudgett,

whose name suggests the bizarre Americans found often-
est in novels written by British authors. His claim of
twenty-seven murders is held to be excessive, but Mr.
Mudgett seems correctly to have felt that his was no
manner of name for one embarking upon such a career,
and therefore rose to fame under the hard pencilian style
of "H. H. Holmes."

It may seem that I have, one after another, excluded
from the field of the collector about every kind of murder, and then proceeded to quote glittering exceptions to
my rules. That is the impression which I get from reading over what I have written. But it should be observed
that all the exceptions either have that element of mystery which "ought to colour every judicious attempt at
murder," or possess some other feature to lift them out
of the ruck. They are, by virtue of this, proper addi-
tions to any collection, however critically chosen. A
mistaken acquittal, an unjust or doubtful conviction and
punishment, a verdict of "not proven," all of these, as
well as that jewel of jewels, the absolutely unexplained
and undetected murder, furnish the necessary mystery
which brightens the collector's eye and makes his heart
to sing.

Is it not time, say you, for me to bring forward some
pure murderers, some who do not transgress the rules?
Well, there is Dr. Lamson, who in 1881 boldly ad-
ministered poison to his victim, *in the presence of a
witness*. There is Miss Constance Kent, already mentioned, who has a further distinction in that the detective
who investigated this murder is said to have been the
original for Sergeant Cuff in "The Moonstone," a novel

still one of the best of detective stories, and saturated with the spirit of murder, although only one, or at most, two, homicides actually occur in the course of it. There is the Unknown Man who committed the murder for which Oscar Slater is at the present moment unjustly suffering. Unjustly, in the opinion of Sir Arthur Conan Doyle, whose book on the subject, as well as the account of the trial (in the Notable British Trials series), seems to me to establish the fact of a miscarriage of justice. There are two New York specimens separated by thirty or forty years in time: the Nathan murder and the Patrick murder. There is the Bram case—murder on the high seas. There is the murder of Dr. Parkman by Professor Webster—a little frayed after seventy years of service as the classic American murder. Hundreds of European and English fanciers have added this to their collections, and you could almost think, after reading some foreign writers, that we had never produced any murderer worthy of attention since the days of Professor Webster! And there is that clear unwavering star of the first magnitude, as plainly the premier amongst American murders as the Madeleine Smith in Scotland, the case of—but space is wanting to describe a masterpiece which I hope later to discuss in something approaching an adequate manner.

It is important, in passing, to remark upon the admirable examples of murder, from the collector's viewpoint, which Scotland has afforded. Or is it merely an apparent eminence due to the interest which her writers show in the subject? Her most famous murderer of modern times, William Burke, came from the neighboring island.

But whatever the cause, the fact is testimony to the law-abiding spirit of the Scotch; only where murder is the exception is it worthy of notice. In countries where everyone is shooting, stabbing, and engaging in assassination, no murders can happen worth five minutes' attention. From Sir Walter Scott, through Stevenson and Andrew Lang, to Mr. Roughead, Scotch writers have collected murders with enthusiasm, diligence and a nice taste. The theme runs through Stevenson's novels like a scarlet thread. There is the murder of Sir Danvers Carew by Mr. Hyde—would that I could see it once more enacted on the stage by Richard Mansfield! It runs through the "New Arabian Nights" and "Treasure Island"; a famous murder is one of the chief incidents in "Kidnapped." Murder stalks abroad in "The Merry Men" and in "Markheim." It is found in "Weir of Hermiston"; its spirit is in "The Ebb Tide" and "The Beach of Falesá." And who that has once read "The Wrecker" can forget the moment when the crew of the *Currency Lass* run up to the deck of Captain Trent's ship into "the dusky blaze of a sunset red as blood"? Scotland offers magnificent opportunities for the collector; it was the sure instinct of genius which laid the scene of the greatest drama in English in that country, and made its King and Queen hero and heroine in that mighty tragedy whose theme is murder.

American writers, with two great exceptions, have tended to neglect this subject. These are Poe and Mark Twain. It must have been noted that there were certain points of resemblance between the murder in "The Black Cat" and the deed of Dr. Crippen; life again modelled itself upon art, as it is said to do. In Mark Twain's books, one recalls the extraordinary scene in the grave-yard in "Tom Sawyer," and the climax of "Pudd'nhead Wilson." In the latter novel, by the way, the fingerprint clew made perhaps its second appearance in fiction. Mark Twain had already employed it, in "Life on the Missis-sippi." Hawthorne seems strangely to have neglected murder—although I believe there is a murder in "The Marble Faun." This was a curious omission for

> The furtive soul whose dark romance
> By ghostly door and haunted stair,
> Explored the dusty human heart
> And the forgotten garrets there.

The subject of the English novelists and poets is too vast even to enter upon, although it may be said that Dickens was at the very height of his powers when he commenced the novel which centres upon murder. Persons who look with contempt upon "The Mystery of Edwin Drood," and the controversy whether a murder was actually committed or only planned, will never attain a degree of intelligence sufficient to become respectable enthusiasts upon murder.

I have heard some prig or other say—or I have read in his writings—that all known murderers are stupid, because the intelligent ones are never discovered. As well pretend that no pictures are good except those never painted; no songs are fine except the ones never written nor sung. Of course, we may long for the perfect, the unattainable murder which flees before our approach, as the lover in Locker-Lampson's "Unrealized Ideal" saw in his dreams the face of the maiden never looked upon in waking hours. Somebody—Stevenson, probably—says that certain places seem to cry aloud for a murder; and the investigating gentlemen in Mr. Machen's "Three Impostors," coming upon the empty house, fall prey to its dismal suggestions. "Here," says one of them, "where all is falling into dimness and dissolution, and we walk in cedarn gloom, and the very air of heaven goes mouldering to the lungs, I cannot remain commonplace. I look at that deep glow on the panes, and the house lies all enchanted; that very room, I tell you, is within all blood and fire."

Only through the omniscience of the novelist may we learn the sensations of the undiscovered murderer. One such tale was for a long time on my list of lost stories; I had read it, and I remembered where and when, but not for a dozen years could I find it once more. It is one of the best bits of murder fiction I know: "The Curate of Churnside," by Grant Allen. The Curate, a delicate-handed Oxonian, named Walter Dene, decided that for his own prosperity and happiness it was necessary for him to remove his uncle, the Vicar. He did it with resolution and precision, and lived happily ever after. Readers, says the author, who thought that he must feel remorse his whole life long were "trying to read their own emotional nature into the wholly dispassionate character of Walter Dene."

The study of murder is the study of the human heart in its darkest, strangest moments. Nothing surpasses it in interest; the little social problems which agonize the heroines of the average novel make their characters seem pallid indeed beside a Lady Macbeth or a Constance

Kent. There comes a time in the experience of such folk when their eyes look upon the smoke of the nether pit. Much of modern fiction pretends to despise such a subject as murder, while it dabbles its feeble hands in cup-and-saucer sentiment, or else in the sham realism of the kitchen-sink.

Of no such pitiful stuff is woven the tale of murder. Nothing pale and thin went to the texture of that story in which the woman looked above her at the ceiling and saw the slowly increasing stain of blood on the plaster; or that in which the two friends went to the room of their enemy to keep Christmas Eve together; or that of the woman who lay awake in the dead hours after midnight and heard the foot-steps of her lodger as he came tip-toeing softly, stealthily, down-stairs, and out by the door. Not less fascinating because it occurred in real life, rather than in imagination, was the moment when the slayer of Miss Gilchrist walked calmly along the passage, up to and past the persons who had surprised him at his work, and then out into the darkness forever; or when the two little old ladies, with their gifts of cake and wine, stood timidly ringing the door-bell outside the apartment where Mr. Rice was being done to death. And there are thousands from whose minds will never wholly vanish the spectacle of old Andrew Borden, walking slowly toward his home under the blinding heat of an August noonday. He reaches his home, and is welcomed therein, but never did any wretched creature step more haplessly into a slaughter-house. His wife already lies murdered, and his own time of life rides upon the dial's point.